Four Letters to the
Witnesses of My Childhood

RELIGION, THEOLOGY, AND THE HOLOCAUST
Steven T. Katz, *Series Editor*

Four Letters
to the Witnesses of My Childhood

. . . .

HELENA GANOR

SYRACUSE UNIVERSITY PRESS

The paper used in this publication meets the minimum requirements of
American National Standard for Information Sciences—Permanence of Paper
for Printed Library Materials, ANSI Z39.48–1984.∞™

For a listing of books published and distributed by Syracuse University Press,
visit our Web site at

SyracuseUniversityPress.syr.edu

ISBN-13: 978-0-8156-0869-1   ISBN-10: 0-8156-0869-1

Library of Congress Cataloging-in-Publication Data
Ganor, Helena.
    Four letters to the witnesses of my childhood / Helena Ganor. — 1st ed.
        p. cm. — (Religion, Theology, and the Holocaust)
    ISBN 978-0-8156-0869-1 (hardcover : alk. paper)
    1. Ganor, Helena.   2. Ganor, Helena—Correspondence.   3. Jewish
children in the Holocaust—Poland—Personal narratives.   4. Holocaust,
Jewish (1939–1945)—Poland—Biography.   I. Title.
DS134.72.G36A3 2007
940.53'18092—dc22
[B]
    2007032502

To my grandchildren,
Jonathan, Michael, David, and John

One writes only half the book; the other half is with the reader.
        —Joseph Conrad, letter to Cunningham Graham

A belief in a supernatural source of evil is not necessary; men alone are quite capable of every wickedness.
        —Joseph Conrad, *Under Western Eyes*

Helena Ganor was born in Lvov in southeastern Poland (now the Ukraine) and lived in Warsaw after World War II. After earning an M.D. degree in 1957, she practiced internal medicine in Warsaw. In 1969 she emigrated to the United States with her husband and two daughters, settling in southern California in the foothills of the San Gabriel Mountains. She recently retired from the practice of medicine. She was awarded second prize for her poetry by the International Society of Poetry.

Contents

❖   ❖   ❖   ❖

Illustrations

. . . .

Acknowledgments

◆　◆　◆　◆

I am grateful to my husband Jan, who was first to read my "letters" and so compassionately shared my emotions, and for his insistence that I save my memories from oblivion.

I would like to express words of gratitude to my talented and wise friend Merrill Joan Gerber for her encouragement, advice, friendly criticism, and assistance in paving the way for the publication of this book.

My thanks also to Ellen Goodman and the staff at Syracuse University Press for their guidance in the preparation of my work for publication.

Introduction

. . . .

I am seventy-one years old and have been writing this memoir
for a few years now—in my imagination, that is. This is the time
to put it on paper before my memories fade away. No, I am not
going to type or write it on a computer, so mistakes can be easily erased or corrected. I will leave a large margin on each page,
so I can add, correct, or subtract whatever I feel I need to do.
In my primitive and sentimental way I am convinced that there
is a magic that happens between the brain (the seat of the human soul), the hand, the pen, and the paper, between the writer
and the reader, that cannot be trusted to modern technology.
I would offer all my earthly treasures for a handwritten letter
from you, Mama. I would imagine your hand holding it, I would
imagine your smile or tears or you sitting and writing it to me.
That connection would be irreplaceable. A letter would convey
the closeness of your fingerprints on the paper despite the years
that have passed by. It would warm my being with a closeness
and intimacy with you.

To be sure, I have nothing against modern advances or technology. I am in awe of all the possibilities that science now has
to offer. It may one day conquer forever the biases and prejudices
of the dark ages and elevate the human brain to the pedestal

where it belongs. That is my highest dream. I still remember and always will cherish the exhilaration I felt on a warm evening in Rome, when, having only a few lire to spend for a soft drink at the neighborhood drugstore, I watched a man walk on the surface of the moon. I remember my lofty pride in the human spirit. I cried then, and I still have, nearly forty years later, an almost unexplainable feeling of joy, bringing tears and hope that suffering and cruelty may one day be erased from our history. But maybe not.

A few months ago, I read two books. The first one, *The Blank Slate: The Modern Denial of Human Nature,* by Steven Pinker, confirmed me in my old belief that there is no such thing as a "blank slate" in the human brain—that no matter what the environmental influences are, we all have innate possibilities for good or evil doings. The second, *The Seven Daughters of Eve,* by Bryan Sykes, brought me again the man-on-the-moon feeling of amazement and excitement of science discovering nature's work. It turns out that the science of genetics can trace the origins of 260 million people of Europe to seven mothers. What a feast!

I am reading a lot these days, books that I never had the chance or time to read. Now that I am 99 percent retired from my professional and motherhood jobs, I read books by novelists, philosophers, and poets, biographies of geniuses, history. I am fascinated by the cave paintings of the Cro-Magnon people, the beauty of them and most of all the need for beauty by those who lived forty to fifty thousand years ago. These people may not have known the connection between mating and giving birth to offspring, so why did their souls need the images of animals they met, they killed, and they ate? Maybe this was the most tender and elevated way to say, "Thank you." Of course I don't know the reasons for their art, but it touches me deeply. Kinship with these men or women seems natural and close. Thousands of years seem to separate us, but really we are alike.

In recent years, I've read Plato, Socrates, Hippocrates, Maimonides, Spinoza, Paine, and Nietzsche. I've explored the history of languages; our Indo-European ancestry; the writings of Thomas Aquinas; the origins of shiny, glorious amber; all that is currently known about our Milky Way and other galaxies; the theory of endless parallel universes; the projected burnout of our sun; and the history of religions. All this and more I read to understand what we are made of. In the end, after absorbing all of this knowledge, I think of myself as an optimistic fatalist. It seems oxymoronic, but really it is not. I am hopeful that we can understand ourselves—by "we" I mean humanity. I also think it will take ages of evolution to unwire what is wired and coded in our genes to transform the primitive impulses of our ancestors to higher purposes—to urges beyond simple fight or flight. I do believe, on the basis of what is known to this point, that Nature has no purpose. It just *is*. We, I, all individuals have to give our lives a purpose. Compared to cosmic time, our lives are milliseconds or less; I leave it to the mathematicians to determine how much less. For myself, I see the purpose of my life as: (1) to be compassionate to all life's creatures; (2) never to be indifferent to suffering, for I consider indifference to be the worst of humanity's flaws; (3) to promote to the best of my ability reason and knowledge against dogmas—any dogmas— that keep us humans in darkness, a darkness that promotes fear and hate; (4) to admire the beauty of our planet and the beauty of our creations—our art, science, philosophy, language; and (5) to learn from our mistakes, both those of our common history and the individual mistakes we make when we do not comply with the preceding four tenets. How much better our short lives would be if we did comply!

One day in 1980, while driving down a mountain ridge, I stopped to admire the green valley below and jotted this little poem on a scrap of paper:

What's life?
A resurrected tree in springtime,
The smell of a dead tree's sap,
A seed that dreams to be awakened,
A night that ends in dawn,
A wind that's born at sea,
A wind that whispers love to me.

When I came home I added a few more verses:

A sip of brandy,
A kick in the ass,
An anger, curse, rebellion, revolution,
Compassion, tenderness and sweat of love,
Intolerance and frolic thoughts,
An esoteric sense of wisdom,
A walk at night and loneliness,
Desire, children's laughter and omnipotent will to live.
This endless inventory,
Does it belong to me?
I still don't know . . . maybe.

♦ ♦ ♦ ♦

Much is made of the meaning of a spiritual life. I contend that
we are all in it together, on this "microscopic" planet called
Earth. Independently of how we came to be, we are here to help
ourselves and others to survive. So far, the only plausible scien-
tific fact is our evolution from the primordial soup of matter to
one cell and then to the complicated biological mechanisms all
around us. Thus evolved, the human brain is the beginning of
everything I hold supreme: the seat of language and writing, the
seat of memory and curiosity, the seat of the "soul" and thus the
eternal seat of good and vice, the seat of intelligence and logi-
cal reason, the seat of awe and beauty. That supreme apparatus,

the brain, created art and philosophies, myths and religions, as ways to understand the unknown. It created architecture, from the ancient Acropolis to modern Bilbao. It created agriculture. It created technology, from the wheel to the computer chip and the double helix of our life's coding. How can one deny that striving to understand the living cell or an atom, the Milky Way or the very universe, *is* the spiritual life of humans? If at the end of the road of all the theories of the universe there is an old bearded man who created it all, well, so be it, but I doubt it. Until then, however, the spiritual life of humans should be that road. The afterlife holds no interest for me, and the world would be better off if we all did our best here and now without expecting any reward when we turn to dust. So here is my road, with its twists and turns through darkness and light.

Historical Timeline

◆ ◆ ◆ ◆

August 23,1939	Germany and Russia sign the Nazi-Soviet Nonaggression Pact, which sets the stage for World War II by ending the Germany's fear of fighting a war on two fronts.
September 1939	On September 1, Germany invades Poland. On September 29, Germany and Russia divide Poland along the rivers Bug and San, with the west occupied by Germany and the east by Russia.
June 1941	Germany attacks Russia; the Russian army withdraws rapidly from eastern Poland.
November 1941	German authorities establish a Jewish ghetto in the city of Lvov, Poland.
1941–43	Beginning in December 1941, Germans systematically deport or liquidate all but 300 of the 120,000 Jews formerly living in the Lvov ghetto.
February 1945	At the Yalta Conference, Franklin D. Roosevelt, Winston Churchill, and Joseph Stalin establish new borders for Poland that

	make eastern Poland (including Lvov) part of the Ukrainian Soviet Republic.
May 1945	The unconditional surrender of German forces to the Allies ends the war in Europe.

Four Letters to the
Witnesses of My Childhood

Letter to My Mother

* * * *

Dear Mama,

You were the first witness of my life, you gave me life. You never expected that our life together would last only eleven years. How could you know it? How could you know what would happen? But let me start from the beginning, what I remember about you and what I cherish in my memory about you.

My memories go back to the time when I was about three to four years old. They are not sequential in time; they are pictures. I remember your images and your words, intermingled with what you told me when I was a little older. Chronology is not that important. What's important is what I know about you and why I love you after more than sixty years have passed by. There was this little town called Warez (or Varyazh, or Varenge), with a square in the middle of it, flanked on each side by little shops owned mostly by Jews. There was a hardware shop where an old, bearded Jew sold nails, horseshoes (I know because he gave me one shiny horseshoe as a gift for good luck) and other mysterious utensils he sold to peasants living in the vicinity. There was an ice cream shop, where children went on hot summer days to buy their treats for a few "groshies"—a grosz equaled a penny, one hundred of them equaled one zloty. The same store sold stamps, candies, and toys. I was probably six when I was a customer of theirs. Another shop which I remember was owned by distant relatives of yours who sold fabrics—we visited them often, although instinctively I knew that the women there didn't like you. Some years afterward, our fates, those of your distant relatives and mine, would intertwine in a terribly tragic way. But I will tell you about it later. For then, I was happy to visit them, although I remember they called me *goyka*, a sarcastic term used by Orthodox Jews to mean a gentile girl. I learned much later that these relations really disapproved of you, not me. You didn't follow the rules: you were educated, you were an atheist, and, even worse, you married one too.

In this little town, there were two churches, one Catholic where Polish peasants went to masses, and the other Russian Orthodox, where all the Ukrainian peasants prayed. There was also a synagogue for Jewish townspeople. With my different friends, I visited all the houses of worship—they were mysterious places where people did mysterious things and made mysterious gestures, sang mysterious songs in languages I couldn't understand—Latin, Ukrainian, and Hebrew; they knelt in front of crosses and paintings of somber figures and chalices and arcs. The one thing I remember is that all of those people never smiled, so I thought they were not very happy there, and it was not much fun for me.

When I was little, probably three years old or less, we lived in a place rented from a man and his wife who had a slaughterhouse next to our house. On the other side of our building was a pharmacy, whose owner and wife always called you "*Frau* doctor." It sounded strange to me—I thought they should call you "*mamusia*," Mommy, like I did. In our house there was a dining room with a big round table and an oil lamp with a beautiful green lamp shade (we called it *abajour*) in the middle of it. There was no electricity in this town. There was a bedroom for you and Father, a little room for me, a kitchen, and the biggest room was the doctor's office, where Father was seeing his patients late into the night. My sister Janka, ten years older than I, lived in a big city where she went to school. You told me stories and read fairy tales to me by the green oil lamp. I thought it was the best time of the day. You also told me how much you wanted to have me and Janka, and how you were full of excitement and couldn't wait to bring us home from the hospital in the big city of Lvov. In that city—also known as Lwów in Polish and Lviv in Ukrainian—I later learned, you had a very hard time bringing me into this world and you almost died. As a little girl, I always thought, not knowing much about this process, how hard could that be? Why didn't I help you, and just "walk out of your body" and be there ready for life and your love?

I don't remember when exactly you and father started to build a new house for us, but I remember holding your warm hand and walking on a summer night with you, toward a big house, full of lights coming out from all the windows. This was the first time I saw electric lights, and they illuminated a big field in front of the house. Stars on the dark sky could be seen only faintly in this glow. You told me then that it was our new house and that was where we were going to live from then on. The house was two-storied with three entrances, with big windows and beautiful wooden and crystal glass entry doors. It had an electric motor, which I was told was named a dynamo. In the left wing of the house was a big waiting room for my father's patients, his office, two examining rooms, an X-ray room that we called the *roentgen* room (where I was never allowed to be), and a special dark room for developing *roentgen* pictures. This last room was the one you worked in. You told me that you traveled far away, to Warsaw, the capital, to go to a special school to become an X-ray technician. William Konrad Roentgen was a German physicist after whom roentgenology was named. He discovered X-rays and won a Nobel Prize for it in 1901. How unusual a woman you must have been for that time! You broke from the orthodoxy of your family, you were educated, you worked, you had children—you were one of those precious humans much ahead of your time. I now know how rare that was in the country in which we lived.

In the middle of the house was a huge dining room—at least from the perspective of my little body it seemed huge to me. In the entrance to this part of the house was a big hall, and when you turned right, there was a big kitchen and pantry. From the kitchen, the doors opened to a never-ending garden with apple trees, plum trees, cherry trees, and boysenberry bushes. This was my playground and paradise. There was the endless hustling and chirping of the birds in the trees, and frogs squawking in the pond, and sometimes wild hares would visit with me. I was learning about the world around me and would come to you asking childish questions about this world. You answered. You were a storyteller, and this is what I remember best from this time of my childhood: you were softness and goodness personified. You had soft hands when you touched me, blue eyes like the sea, in which I drowned falling asleep in your arms. You gave me life twice—but that's another story that I will tell you later.

Let's go back to this new house. On the second floor of the house there were three bedrooms: mine, my sister's, and yours, and a big "salon"—what I would now call a living room. The salon had a grand piano on which Father sometimes played, and when he played I saw a smile on your face or tears in your eyes—I didn't understand why, but now I do—this was another gift from you, a gift of sharing tender feelings.

Each room had a tiled warming stove, tall, reaching the ceiling, each of a different color, and in the winter evenings, our maid, Handzia, would light up the coals in those beautiful fireplaces to warm up the bedrooms.

The salon opened onto a big terrace—I would call it now a patio or balcony—in which you planted in big wooden pots pink and white oleanders, which bloomed in midsummer. You know, I now have big bushes of oleander in my garden in California, and although they are very ordinary flowers here, they are still as exotic to me as they were to you when you tended them and cared for them, placing them inside the house during the harsh, snowy winter.

During hot summers I remember a colorful spectacle coming to our town—the Gypsies. Ah, the Gypsies! They came in painted wagons drawn by horses; the wagons were built like little houses with windows and doors, and chimneys on the top. I always wished I could have one like that and live in it. They were painted with pictures of valleys, all green with flowers growing in them and animals running through them. The skies over the valleys were stark blue and here and there white clouds were passing over them—it was magic to me and I remember asking you why our house couldn't be painted like this. I don't remember what you answered, but I was left to be satisfied that our house "sparkled" in the sunlight—it had in its paint something like mica, so it had some magic in it too. I envied the Gypsy children because they were free to do whatever they wanted all day long; they didn't have to wash themselves every day, and they ate only when they were hungry. I made friends with those little boys and girls, and we would run together to the river far beyond the town and splash in the water. I stayed close to the banks because I didn't know how to swim, but the Gypsy children were always swimming, some of them even disappearing under the water for a few seconds and then coming up shaking their black hair with drops sparkling around their heads like silver haloes. One day a woman came to you and told you that I shouldn't be playing with "those *tzygans*" (*tzygans* was a Polish name for Gypsies) because they were known to steal children and take them away with them. When I asked you if it was true, you told me not to worry; you told me that they have plenty of children of their own and they don't need more. You allowed me to play with them. I believed you and thought you were the best Mama ever to allow me such happy pleasures. There was one more "adventure" the Gypsy children introduced me to. In our garden grew a huge mulberry tree (*morva* in Polish), just on the border with the Ukrainian church. The branches of this tree spread out from the main trunk close to the ground, and it was easy to climb. Aping my summer friends' skills, I climbed with them high into the tree, so high that we could see the inside of the church abutting our garden through the windows. The mulberries we picked were yellowish with some fuzzy hair on them and sweeter than sugar. We ate them until our tummies were full and I brought some of the high tree trophies to you. You probably pretended to like them, and I was very proud of my adventure's gift. I'm telling you about this summer's delight not only because of my happy memories with my wandering friends, but also because later on in my life they and we shared the common world of hate we did not deserve.

I was about six years old when you and Papa decided I should go to school after the summer. I already knew how to read my books and could write simple words. I also knew how to count up to a thousand. That fall you dressed me up in a special outfit for special occasions: it was a navy blue pleated skirt reaching below my knees and a top that was also navy blue, with a big square collar resting on my shoulders and a little vee neckline in front ending with a short triangular tie. The collar and tie had two embroidered white lines on the edges. It was like a miniature marine's uniform—I guess it was the fashion of the day, made especially for me by the seamstress in the town. I knew it was a special outfit because earlier that year when we traveled to the big city of Lvov to visit my sister Janka, who was going to school there, I was also dressed up in it. I remember this outfit so well because during, our trip to this beautiful city, Papa took us to the most famous photographer there to make a lot of pictures of all of us. One of the pictures showing you and me together the photographer later sent to us in a big framed portrait with his thank you note. It turned out to be a winner in a photographer's exhibition in the big city of Lvov. I'm telling you about this now because this image of you and me is etched in my memory forever—three years later it saved my life. How it happened I will tell you later; it's a story on its own, revealing how innocent and accidental happenings at one time have accidental and profound outcomes in the time ahead. I'm sure it happens to many people at one time or another; it happened to me many times in my life. Remind me dear Mama to tell you about the story of our portrait.

But let's go back to the first and last few days in the school of Warez. The school building was next to the Catholic church. In fact, one had to go through the apse of the church to get to the classroom. After a few days of attending the school, I came home and told you that all the teacher was teaching were things I already knew. The only thing new to me was the paternoster, to be recited after the teacher at the start of the class hour. The prayer was recited in Polish. It started with the words, *"Ojcze nasz ktory jestes w niebie,"* "Our father in Heaven . . . " After my simple report about the teaching, I know you checked the curriculum of the next grade, the second grade of the school, and decided to teach me at home and when the time was right you would send me, like my sister, to a better school in the big city.

So, there I was, free to roam the world of my happy childhood with the best teacher I ever had—you. I'm certain that my present curiosity I owe to you. I remember when playing with numbers I "discovered" that if the sum of a big number, for example 123, equals a number that divides by 3, the whole number is divisible by 3.

When my father went to France to visit the International Exhibition in Paris, I asked you, "What is France?" You told me that there are many countries in the world; Poland is only one of them, and France is another one, far away. Then I asked you who lives there, are they the same people as here? Not knowing what was coming from a child's imagination, you said yes. Oh! I said, that means that the Poles, the Ukrainians, and the Jews live in France. Those were the only people I knew.

I don't remember the expression on your face or the reaction to those "discoveries" of mine, but being a mother myself and an observer and teacher of my children, I can imagine your amazement and pride in both my naïvete and my logic. You let me play and be friends with all the children that I liked. I remember I stayed overnight with my Ukrainian friends Ivoushka and her brother Sasha. They and their whole family used to come to Papa as patients, and as they waited in the waiting room or in their horse-driven wagons I played with them. I slept in their *khatas* (as their houses were called) on a big bed with down and feather covers, with beautiful hand-embroidered flowers on the stiff ironed bed linens. The towels we dried our washed bodies with were also embroidered, with red and black traditional ornaments. Their food was delicious, and the parents of my friends always sent me back with some gifts for you—apples, pears, or berries. We played among the animals of their farm, chased geese, and chickens, and little "baby horses" and "baby cows," as I used to call them. I never could imagine and would never find an explanation for the fact that the same people only a few years later wanted to kill you and me just because we were called Jewish. At that time of my life I didn't even know what *Jewish* meant. I only knew that Jews were people who dressed differently from us: the men wore long black dresses, black hats, and long beards, and on a "Sabbath" (Saturday) night they wore hats brimmed with fur and went to their churches, called synagogues, to pray; the women when they married wore wigs and black handkerchiefs on their heads. My friend Àmele was dressed the same way I was, but her dress was a little longer than mine and I thought it was very pretty and princess-like. One time she invited me to her house for a special holiday dinner. The dinner was served in a tentlike structure that then I knew by its Polish name, *al-tanka*; now I would say it was specially built for that occasion, an outdoor room. Her father built it with branches and twigs, with green leaves still on them. The partial roof was open to the sky, so when their family prayed to their God, the words went straight to Heaven. I didn't stay there too long because unknowingly I made a big mistake and brought my beloved companion, Bambi, with me. He always ate dinner with us, so I thought the invitation included him. Bambi was my friend, a smooth-hair terrier about one foot high, all white with brown ears and paws and a dark patch over one eye. He had a two-inch-long tail, which wagged incessantly when he was happy and playing with me and kept still when he was scolded for disobedience. My sister and I named him Bambi after the little baby deer story, which I read in one of my books. So, as it came to be, Bambi was the reason I didn't participate in the only special holiday dinner I was ever invited to. He didn't want to stay outside the elaborate outdoor room, and so we went home, after I had a few bites of a very tasty meal. Àmele cried when I was leaving, and I couldn't understand why three friends—Àmele, Bambi, and I—couldn't eat this dinner together. I don't remember how you, my sweet protector, explained it to me, but I know it was something consoling and probably ended up with some treats and your warm embraces.

Those are some of the vivid pictures that I retained in my memory, witnessed by you in this almost idyllic space of my life. Some other episodes known to you I will describe in the letters to Papa and Janka, where you were only a bystander even though an important one and dear to my soul.

I want to tell you what I learned about you almost twenty years after I lost you forever from my life. I learned that your maiden name was Machla Clara Lorberbaum; that your roots were Ashkenazim, which means the tribes of Semites traveling after Diaspora from the land of Israel via Turkey to northern and eastern Europe; and that my great-grandmother's name was Balaban, which is of Turkish origin. Your mother, sister, and brother, who emigrated to Palestine in 1922, adopted the surname of Daphne as their family name, translating literally the "Lorberbaum" of German origin and giving it back to Greek and Hebrew origin.

What else can I tell you I remember from this faraway time, more than half a century ago? Sometimes certain colors and smells unwind in my memory, bringing back vivid experiences. I see myself running in the summer day through a field of ripened wheat, its color blending with the color of my hair, woven in two braids, reaching halfway to my waist. I knew exactly where to run, because when I stretched my body and stood on the tips of my toes, I could spot this unforgettable combination of colors: shining bright red of poppies (*maki* in Polish) and intense blue puffs of bachelor's buttons (*blawatki*) swaying and drowning in the sea of gold. My friends and I picked those flowers and wove them into wreaths to beautify our heads with flower tiaras. Now whenever I see it in my mind's eye, it is a scene from a fairy tale. No wonder it got recorded into my brain forever. Sometime later, when the red petals of the poppies withered away, their fruits would show up as light brown hard bulbs, about four or five centimeters in diameter, topped with a ragged, rough button. When we shook those poppy bulbs, they made noise like Spanish castanets or Mexican maracas. We would break off this top button and pour the poppy seeds into our mouths—we loved it.

The smell brings out another memory, the scent of burning candles in the middle of a snowy and cold winter, when we had in our house a decorated pine tree called a *choinka,* which was really a Christmas tree. It never in those days had any connection with any specific holiday or religious event in my consciousness—I thought it was a celebration of winter, just as the poppy wreaths celebrated summer and huge bouquets of lilacs celebrated spring. I don't remember the exact timing of the lit candles on our tree, but I know that my Polish and Ukrainian friends had the same trees with candles at different times, almost two weeks apart. The smell of food at this time of my life was never attractive or enticing. I didn't like to eat and was a very skinny girl, which I know worried you. The only things I liked were eggs in any form, tomato soup, fresh rolls with crunchy crusts that our maid and cook Handzia baked herself, and fruits and berries, which tasted the best when I picked them myself. There was a lot of persuading, coaxing, and cajoling on your part, gentle and otherwise, going on for me to eat. Sometimes you would let me sit at the table for a long time after everybody finished dinner, hoping that was punishment enough for me to clean the food from the plate. But most often than not, I won—if I didn't like it, I didn't eat it, and you would give up and comply with my taste. On these occasions Papa would say that you spoiled me, but I loved you for it.

I was also a very shy girl and would hide away when guests or family would come to visit—it would take me some time to warm up to them or talk to them. As funny as it sounds, I was the most gregarious and companionable when they were at the door saying their good-byes.

If I scratched the pages of my memory a little longer, I could probably write some more about my first seven years of life—the years you witnessed—but it wouldn't change the image of serenity that I retained from those years, serenity that nourished my thoughts, if only subliminally, during the very dark times and gave me strength to hope that one day in the future, I'd be back in this peaceful place.

◆　◆　◆　◆

Soon after my seventh birthday, peril entered our lives. On September 1, 1939, an enemy—the Germans—attacked our country, and without much effort proceeded fast and entered Warsaw, pushing swiftly eastward toward us. Of course now I know very well the history and the political climate, internal and external, of those times. But at that time, I only knew the word *war*. I knew it was something to be afraid of. Suddenly in one night everything changed for me, for us, for everybody. On that one dark night, you woke me, dressed me in warm clothes, and took me outside of our house, where, in the darkness of a moonless night, there stood a horse-driven wagon packed with hay and a peasant sitting on a little wooden bench on the front and holding the reins of the horses in his hands. He was ready to drive me away.

My uncle, Papa's oldest brother, was standing there and waiting for me. I knew him only from occasional visits in the big city of Lvov where he lived. He was a very tall and lanky man, with sunken cheeks, big eyes, grayish hair and moustache, and very long, skinny arms. A bachelor, he lived alone in a darkish city apartment and taught in a *gymnasium,* as high school was called. He was never affectionate, and not much warmth emanated from him, as I remembered from our infrequent visits to Papa's family in Lvov.

You kissed me and embraced me hurriedly, you told me not to be scared, that I'd be safe with my uncle, not to cry or talk loudly, and most of all you repeated many times that we would be together in a couple of days. There was a nestlike place made for us in the pile of hay, lined with a blanket, where my uncle and I settled. The "hay cave" was big enough for me to lie down, but Uncle Kazik—the diminutive form of his full name, Kazimierz, a Polish royal name—had to bend his knees so his feet wouldn't stick out of our nest. Over our heads there were four panels of wood arranged in an inverted vee shape, covered with a thin layer of straw. In any other time, it would be a dream adventure, but on this fateful night it was eerily ominous and with my awakening intuition, I knew it was not a children's play. I heard the driver order the horses: Veeio! The horses jerked the wagon into motion, and in a steady trot we were moving on forward on a bumpy road. Uncle Kazik held my left hand in his right one and with the other one petted my forehead and cheeks. He whispered sweet things to me. At this moment he was an extension of your love and tenderness and I felt safe and warm, even in those weird circumstances. After some short time the bumpy road turned into a paved one, and the ride was smoother, with a faint noise of the wheels as they turned, tediously uniform. My eyes were fixed on the sky, which I could see through the gaps of hay and straw—it was black with an unsymmetrical design of sparkling polka dots of the stars. Why all this mystery? Why escape? Why fear? After a while I was surprised that I actually had fun; it was mysterious and eerie and I thought in my childish imagination that maybe you arranged it all in your generosity, for me to have fun, so I shouldn't fail to fulfill your expectation and disappoint you.

Then, suddenly the wagon stopped and we heard loud voices of several men asking our driver in Ukrainian what was he carrying in his wagon. He told them he was going to Sokal, a small city, about halfway between our town and Lvov, and that he was taking a supply of hay and straw to a relative who lived there. The men knew him and called him by his first name. They told him he could go. They were looking for Jews who were trying to escape to the other side of the river Bug (pronounced "Boogh") and over the "border," which ran between our little town of Warez and Sokal, the first leg of our journey to Lvov. Their voices were nervously excited, sometimes lowering to a hissing whisper. They told him how they would help the Germans to finish off all the Jews and get rich in the process. The driver kept the secret; he didn't tell them about his cargo. He had already gotten a lot of money for his service. I imagine he was thinking slyly that he would be doubly lucky when upon his return from his mission he would join them in their lofty plans.

My dearest Mama, those could have been the same people that you took care of when Papa delivered their babies and you tended to their wives; the same people whose tuberculosis-ravaged lungs you took X-rays of and who you helped by draining the suppurating content from their chests so they could heal and breathe; the same people that you fed when they were hungry after a long trip to see the doctor; the same people who, if they didn't have the money, paid for all of the care with whatever they could—with chickens, eggs, or potatoes—or didn't pay at all; the same people who bent and bowed with deep gratitude to both of you with a simple *"Boje tiebya khrany,"* God bless you; the same people whose children were my friends and whom I visited in their houses to play and sleep under their roofs; the same people who lined the road and threw flowers in front of Papa when he was returning from a long absence to the town, in radiant joy that "their doctor" was back; the same people who on Sunday mornings, before going to the church next door, would come and talk to you about their children, their joys and their sorrows, soliciting your good heart to be on their side; the same people who beat their wives and children in a drunken stupor and then brought them to our house for consolation and care; the same people that I felt we, you and I, were part of and one with. I soon learned, however, that I was different, although for a long time I failed to understand why. It took me a lifetime to connect the dots, between the wretchedness of evil souls and spontaneous unjustified hate, between inferiority complexes and overwhelming desire for power, between the stupidity of cruelty and the pleasures derived from it, and to understand the nobility of wisdom, of everything that is opposite of the above.

The dawn was about to break, painting everything in grayish colors with a hint of pink, when we stopped in front of a small house. The driver helped us to get out of our "hay cave," mumbled something, turned around, and went back where he came from.

We slept in this house until the next evening and then boarded a train, no luggage, no suitcases. After a few stops on the way, we arrived in Lvov—the big city I knew vaguely. There, my other uncle, the younger brother of Papa, whose name was Youzek (a diminutive of Youseph or Joseph—this time a biblical name!) took us to his house. He was tall, a little pudgy, with light blond hair and blue eyes. He was an architect; he had a wife and also two daughters like you: Halinka (from Halina) and Evunia (from Eva), who was a little younger than I. I stayed there some days—I don't remember exactly how many—but after that separation from you, which seemed like an eternity, you came and said, "We are going home," not to the house I knew but our new house.

Memory is a curious thing. Sometimes the details are erased as if somebody had taken a wet sponge and cleaned the slate and one only remembers the main event; sometimes, however, one remembers all the minute details, seemingly not important, culminating in some grand picture. The main event at this point was seeing your half-smiling face and feeling your warm hand holding mine, and opening the door of our new "house." How we got there has been erased.

Our new home was an apartment in an eight-story building; the building was dark gray, the first two floors occupied by a big restaurant, very chic and elegant, called Europejska, which means European. Our apartment was on the sixth floor. It had three bedrooms, one living room, one bathroom, a long corridor leading to each of those rooms, and one room—the darkest of them all—probably for a maid. It was situated at the corner of the building, so the windows on one side showed the street on which the building stood. The street's name was Ulica 3-go Maja, 3rd of May Street, named to commemorate the date of the constitution of the nation to which we thought we belonged. On the other side, the windows opened to a view of a green expanse as far as the eye could see—it was a park about half a block away named after a Polish hero, Tadeusz Kosciuszko. I wonder if you knew that he also played a part in the American revolution.

That was the place where for the next year and a half my life would be centered.

Why all this change? Why a new home? Why escape from the place of my carefree childhood? The explanation is very simple and at the same time very, very complicated—two of the most infamous people of the century, competitors of Olympic proportions desiring absolute power and having a degenerate philosophy of cruelty came together and signed a pact. This happened on August 23, 1939—exactly one week before the Germans crossed the border of Poland. This was the so-called pact of nonaggression between Adolf Hitler, the chancellor of the Third Reich, and Joseph Stalin, the ruler of the Soviet Union. Their goals and aims were different, but their political perfidy was perfectly matched. As a result, our country was arbitrarily divided between those two "neighbors"—and our lives changed forever, never to be the same again.

The details of that time are written in thousands of history books. But this is my story, and a story about you, the precious witness to my life. This much will suffice for the purpose of this letter.

I recall a sentence I once read in a book—I think it was Raymond Chandler who wrote it, or possibly André Gide. When his beloved wife died, he wrote: "I lost a witness to my life; when somebody dies, a library burns." My desire is for the library not to burn, for the library to be frequented with tenderness by my children and grandchildren, and if a tear or a smile is born in that library, then I become an important witness to their lives and maybe make them softer or richer, while I'm lurking in the shadows of the other side of the river Styx. You know, my dear Mama, on that mysterious night of escape, I knew only that we were going to the "big city of Lvov," on the other side of the border, on the east side of the river Bug. Now, many, many years after that night in the peasant's wagon, I took a map to look up those places, the little corner of the world that became my whole world for the next five years of my life, and four of yours. In a very schematic way, to see it more clearly in my mind's eye, I drew a chart of this piece of Earth where we would live and travel through the nightmare of that time, you ending your nightmarish dream in a place of no return. And here it is:

had a beautiful voice and an ear for music; her voice was silky and soft, warm and soothing, with just enough thrill in it to make me feel loved. She inherited this gift from you. Alas, I didn't.

One more episode was not only a first, but also the only one never to be repeated. I was signed up for ballet school, which I attended three times a week; it was located in the municipal opera house. The building looked regal to me and was built as a close copy of the Paris Opera. It stood at the end of a wide, tree-lined boulevard. Mostly girls attended this school. We entered at the side door at the end of the building. The lessons were conducted in the evening and the teacher was a Russian ballerina, who had had her glory days many years ago in the Leningrad Ballet. Her name was Alexandra, but we addressed her as Madame Sasha. We learned the foot and hand positions of classical ballet and different pas, pirouettes, and figures. I loved it. I felt transported to a fairytale world, a world that had no connection to everyday life. A different language reigned there. The pink tutus and pink shoes we wore made us special and unique and so different compared with the outside world. At the end of the year, Madame Sasha chose ten girls, the best in the class, to perform on the real stage of the opera in a production of the ballet *Don Quixote*. And how proud and elated I was—I was one of those girls! We were to dance as flowers in the field, dominated by windmills where the drama between Don Quixote and his beloved Dulcinea was to take place. That evening was magic! Magic enhanced by knowing that you and Papa and Janka were watching me from the enormous dark space with rows of seats filled with people. Of course, I didn't see you, but more than ever before I felt your eternal presence, in every ballet step, as in every step of my life. I knew you were there because I was yours and you were mine.

In May 1941, all the classes came to an end—the real school and the magical one of ballet. The town was teeming with Russian soldiers and officers. The color of their uniforms had a different hue from what I remember of the Polish uniforms. They wore boots of soft leather that wrinkled and folded like accordions, whereas the Polish officers' boots were stiff and shiny, reaching the knee. The caps were round with a red or blue ribbon circling them, and just above a black and shiny visor that shaded their Russian eyes, there was five-armed shiny red star. Sometimes they would stop me on the street and talk to me and pet my cheeks and hair. And I remember one Russian officer who lived in the same building with us—whenever he met me on the stairs he would kiss my forehead and in time translated my name into Russian and called me Lenochka. Maybe I reminded him of his daughter and filled up the gap of his longing and his love.

What I've told you until now, my dear Mama, that is all that I knew about soldiers or about war. Why should I have known more? I was not even nine years old. War is an abstract word to a child. The only thing that permeates the thought of a child is reality. A child reading or listening to a fairytale believes it is reality. When the extremes of reality—the most beautiful experiences and the most horrific ones—descend in unforeseen sequences, the only way to survive is to be armed with a shield of secret places. The secret places one has to learn to visit, as if the darkness is only a fleeting moment and the light at the end of the road is like shiny water flowing without seeming purpose to an endless destiny of the ocean.

Something nervous was in the air in May 1941: your whispers, your averting your eyes when I looked at you; the silence at the table, the going in and out of the house without telling me where, and silent tears from Clara, who for some time lived with us. Remember the strange dinner I had in Warez with my friend Àmele and my beloved Bambi? Well, Clara was Àmele's older sister, and daughter of that old, bearded Jew who once gave me a shiny horseshoe for good luck. Clara was about the age of Janka, and you "adopted" her into our family; she was the only one of her big family who escaped from Warez to the east and didn't know a soul on this side of river Bug. I will tell you her story later, because I feel that your generous heart will be warmed by this rare story of a happy ending.

One day you told me that you arranged for me a vacation time in a little town, very much like the one we lived in before, and I would be staying with relatives of yours—a far-removed uncle and aunt, the same ones who used to call me *goyka*. You assured me that it was not far away and that they would take care of me and my summer would be painted again with flowers in the fields and silver waters of the streams. You told me to be polite and call them uncle and aunt and that just before school would start you would bring me back. The name of the town where I was to spend the summer was called Radjekov (Radziechow)—it was the easternmost point of the devil's pitchfork I drew for you earlier. Once I got there, I knew I was destined to see the strangest things from then on. There were three men in this family—one old (the "uncle") and two younger ones—four women—one old one ("the aunt") and three young women—and two children— one boy and one girl. It is sad and maybe even unforgivable that I don't remember their names. The only excuse I have is that events soon to come blotted out their names from my memory. Their quarters were crowded—three rooms, a tiny kitchen, and a tiny yard with chickens running around. The kitchen had an iron stove and two big tables, which I marked in my mind as a "milk table" and "meat table." I was told in stern terms never, never to mix them up, because it was a sin and not according to the law of the Hebrew God. Neither *sin* nor *God* had any meaning to me. I never knew or was told that I was a sinner. The only thing that appealed to me were the songs that the women sang when we were together in one room preparing for sleep. The melodies were a mixture of defiance and submission, of sadness and fear, of longing and disappointment, of failure to fulfill the expectations of hope. Much, much later in my life I understood how those songs reflected their alienation from others. When the sadness was condensed to the point of saturation, there would come a short burst of joy in the song that usually ended abruptly. In the future I felt the same sequence of rhythm in other folk songs.

Before the candles burned out, we would sit in our beds, and the women asked me about the life in our family and to my answers responded outwardly with a kind of exaggerated horror, but I felt the younger ones had eyes full of curious envy. Perhaps, however, all this is just my wishful afterthought.

All of them wore traditional Orthodox clothes, with not much color in them—mostly black, brown, and dark blue—but on special occasions, the women decorated themselves with delicate laces.

On Saturdays, to start the fire in the stove, they had a Christian, or "Gentile," woman to come and light the match to kindle the fire. If I was there and the woman didn't come on time, I again became the *goyka*—the Gentile—appointed to do the job. They probably thought that I was so beyond rescue from their god's revenge that this little sin they made me commit would not tip the scale, which was already out of balance.

The town of Radjekov was a little bigger than the Warez of my childhood. It had the same typical square in the middle of it, with houses one or two stories high on each of the four sides. There was an apothecary that sold some remedies for ailing health, but also ice cream, candies, and toys; there was a post office and, as I was told, some rich people's houses. Only few of the people who lived in the town were not Jewish, although immediately on the outskirts of the town were the houses and farms of Ukrainian and Polish peasants. Most of the Jewish homes had mezuzahs on the frames of their front doors, small scrolls inscribed with an excerpt of Hebrew scripture. Believing that a mezuzah on the door would keep their homes safe and sacred, Orthodox Jews treated it with reverence, kissing it on leaving or entering the house.

I was wandering around the town by myself, not having any friends there, and the only place I knew outside of the town was a peasant's farm and house. The man who lived there used to bring logs and chop them up in suitable sizes for stove and fireplace. I

a class in tolerance.
A wonder of symbolic Sabbath candles,
and sadness of the songs
    belonging to the lost land.
Vacation with blood relatives she didn't know,
With strangers of lost world.
Abruptly all this ended
    with cannons, screams
    and vulgar death.
The "teachers" in black uniforms
announced an intermission
    in the theater of peaceful life.

            ◆   ◆   ◆   ◆

A road to town is dark,
A lonely wooden wagon,
A miserable horse
    encouraged by a whip.
Kilometers go slow,
My girl at mercy of a peasant
With Judas's silver in his fist.
If there was ever Christ,
That's how He must have felt.
Is there a purpose to her death?
Is innocence a sin?
The wagon stops.
Soft touch of mother's hand
    and smell of safety . . .
        short-lasting and elusive band.

The land was seldom free.
The hatred of conquerors and strangers
    was taught for ages
    and passed to children

through DNA.
A vengeful nature's twisting helix
    became a whip
    in inquisition's hand again
We want your bread, they shouted,
    your homes, your children,
    your poets, writers,
    your gold and silver!
She-wolf forgot her children
    and joined the foreign pack.
We want your blood! they shouted,
    and burned, and killed,
    and spat at faces of humanity.
A nightmare of amnesia was around . . .

◆ ◆ ◆ ◆

The next morning I learned new facts, the news I needed to know immediately:

First: Papa was gone. He had been recruited into the Russian army to treat their wounded soldiers at the front. He would be gone for a long time, you told me.

Second: the Germans were in the town, and I was not to wander the streets by myself, and nobody was to go out of the house after dark—it was curfew.

Third: you were working in the same hospital as before, but much longer hours, so I would only see you late in the evening. You and Janka would come home together from work, because she was no longer a medical student, but worked as a nurse in the same hospital with you.

Fourth: I was to stay home and wait for you. If somebody knocked on the door, I was to pretend I was not there.

Fifth: The "adopted" Clara left to go to some other house, to live with some other people. No explanation was given to me, but I soon learned why she left.

Except for Papa being gone "temporarily," as you told me, I didn't care about all the other news and changes, as long as I was with you. I still believed that you had the power to make everything right for us—for me and Janka.

There was a sixth thing that you didn't tell me about. When you and Janka put your coats on in the morning to go to work, I noticed that attached to the right sleeves of your coats was a white band with a blue star painted on it. This time it was a six-pointed star, not five-pointed like the one on Russian soldiers' caps. The star was easy to draw—two triangles, one straight up and the other placed upside down on the first one. I learned that it was called the star of David, or Mogen David in Hebrew. *Mogen* means "shield"; I guess it refers to the shield David wore when he defeated the giant Goliath. This time it was a symbol not of a victory but of defeat and humiliation. I, being less than ten years old, was not forced to wear it. I never did.

When I told you in a nervous, speedy, and confused way what I witnessed in the town of Radjekov, you believed me. Why would you believe me? It should not be believable! In any other times than these, you would have taken your child to the doctor and ask him to cure her from this horrific, sick imagination—but you knew better. You believed me!

◆ ◆ ◆ ◆

All those rules I was to obey became null and void very shortly after my coming back from Radjekov. We were ordered to move to a "ghetto," a word I had never heard before. Suddenly, we became "the Jews." Suddenly we were not Poles anymore. We didn't belong; we were marked for death.

We were allowed to pack our personal belongings, those which fit in a few suitcases. Janka's friend, a young man with whom she worked at the hospital, helped us to pull a small cart with our load, for some kilometers, to our destination. I learned that the ghetto would be a holding place for planned killings, and was soon to be a slaughterhouse for all who entered. That's what it was! That's what it was for us. That is how it should have been defined in every dictionary printed after 1945—but it wasn't.

My dear Mama, if my children or grandchildren picked up any dictionary in my house wanting to know the meaning of the word *ghetto*, all they would learn is that it was "a part of a city in which a minority group lives." They might even learn that the word originated in sixteenth-century Venice, where Jews were segregated and isolated but supposedly lived a very comfortable life. Unless they read this letter to you they would never know about the ghetto I lived in. In honor of you and all the other ghetto inhabitants, I am adding my definition: a holding place for Jewish people, organized by Germans just before the planned slaughter, starving, and annihilation of the Jews—Hitler's "final solution."

In silence and tragic amazement, we passed the center of the city, moving north toward the railroad embankment and entered the territory of the ghetto through a short tunnel under the embankment. The tunnel on both sides was guarded by special German troops called Gestapo; their duty was to make sure that nobody from this slow-moving procession of thousands would escape before being trapped in the ghetto. How it was arranged that we—you, Janka, and me—ended up in a small room together is beyond my power of recollection or even more truthfully, beyond my knowledge—I just didn't know how we ended up in this narrow, long room, as I remember it now. It was about two or three meters wide and eight to nine meters long, with two beds, one table, and a washstand. Over the table you hung a framed photograph portrait of you and me, the same one that long ago was a winner in the artistic photographs exhibition in this town. It was indeed a sweet depiction of mother and child. Our heads were close to each other and our eyes were fixed on your open palm, which held a single pea. My little finger was touching this round seed. The composition was very simple, it was in muted grayish and white colors and it radiated tender love;

it was almost like a Madonna and child by Raphael. The descent from a beautiful, luxurious house to a fairly large and comfortable apartment and then to this room just became a fact of life, a fact of "now" reality. The room was once part of a big apartment with three bedrooms; our room was the last in the *amfilada,* or suite of rooms lying in one line. There was no corridor; to get to our bedroom we had to pass through two bedrooms full of people and make the same trip in reverse if we wanted to go to the bathroom. We used a big chamber pot at night in order not to disturb the other families in the bedrooms in front of us. You and I slept together in one bed, and Janka had the other.

Very early in the morning you left for work in a hospital on the "Aryan" side of the city—the part that was not in the ghetto, where the non-Jews lived. The Germans needed you there as an experienced X-ray technician, so you got a special pass to get in and out of the ghetto. Janka worked as a nurse in the ghetto hospital. Its director, Dr. Litvak, had known Papa before the war, and she always told us how nice he was to her.

I was told never, not ever, to go out on the street by myself. I could go out only with you or my sister. The reason for this was that every few days the German gendarmes organized round-ups on different streets; we called it *lapanka,* from the Polish verb *lapac,* meaning "catch" or "grab." They would close off a few blocks of the street, and whoever was there was grabbed by force and thrown into big military trucks and taken away, never to be seen again. If any of the people tried to escape, they shot them right there and then and threw their bloodied bodies into the trucks together with those still alive. I watched it happening from the only window in our room many times. I heard the screams on the street and saw those people shot if they tried to run away. This was my reality now.

When I stayed alone in this long, narrow room, there were only a few things I could do while waiting for you to come home. There were a few books in the room, but I read only two of them.

One was *Pan Tadeusz,* a long poetic saga by the greatest Polish poet, Adam Mickiewicz, which was much too difficult for me to understand. I enjoyed it only when he painted in beautiful words the forests, the rivers, and the nature that had been part of my life not so long ago but seemed now to be removed by ages. The second book was about the baby deer called Bambi. Was it accident or intuition that led my mother to bring this book to the ghetto with our other few possessions? Bambi, the deer, reminded me of my dog Bambi of our happy days, but I also cried in fear that I might lose you, as Bambi lost his mother.

The other thing I did while waiting for you was to sit on the only windowsill and watch the street. Across the street was a candy factory with a name painted on the wall: Suchard. I guess they were still producing candies, probably for the German army; I know they did because on a breezy day I could catch a whiff, a slight scent of the candies I used to eat ages ago.

But my most pleasurable activity was to "talk" to my friend across the street. There was a house next to the candy factory, and on the first floor lived a boy, about my age, with curly black hair. We never met or talked, but we had this window-to-window friendship; I never even knew his name. He showed me his toys through the window and the books he had; he made clownish faces, and we both laughed; he showed me the food he was going to eat; and once he showed me a big letter *M* written on a piece of paper, so from then on I called him "M-boy." Of course I reciprocated with everything I could say about myself through the window of our friendship. It was like a pantomime theater, a play without words. When I told you about my window friend, you told me you were happy I had him.

We never went to any stores to buy food. You and Janka brought food every evening when both of you came from work. It was always black bread, sometimes chicken, marmalade, potatoes, beets, and milk. You told me neither of you liked the milk, so it was only for me. Sometimes you brought some canned food that tasted different, *ersatz* food produced by the Germans as a substitute for the real thing. I stopped being picky about food. I ate everything, and most of the time I was hungry. I even ate *lebiodka* (wild marjoram), a weed that you would pick up on the side of the road; it tasted like spinach, which I had once hated. Many times, whenever you could, early in the morning before going to work, you would drop me off at a clandestine school organized by a husband and wife who used to be teachers before the war. Children of different ages would gather in their two rooms with curtain-drawn windows, so nobody could see us from the street. In a low voice they read some books to us, or taught us the history of the country we didn't belong to anymore, some basics in geography of places far away with exotic names like Asia, Africa, or America, which I tried to believe really existed. One of the older girls, whose name was Janka Hesheles, organized a theater there, and we all took turns playing some imaginary roles. Her father had been an editor at a most important newspaper in Lvov before the war. All of us were delighted in this imaginary escape from our grim existence. After the war, she published a book about these times, *Oczyma 12-letniej dziewczyny* (Through the Eyes of a 12-Year-Old Girl). I have this book, which I brought with me to America. Papa bought it for me after the war, because she wrote about me, naming me by my first and last name and thus making me more than just an anonymous girl who survived this nightmarish time. This book, as I see it now, was a Polish equivalent of *The Diary of Anne Frank*. How sad it is, my dear Mama, that this book is unknown to the world. It isn't known because this young girl unwittingly showed less than noble picture of the country we once called ours. So its people did not want to "spread the news" and popularize her book.

◆   ◆   ◆   ◆

I promised you earlier that I would tell you a story with a happy ending, so before I recall the most tragic time in my life, I'll tell you the story of Clara, your "adopted" young woman, the one who lived with us after escaping from Warez to Lvov. You knew the reason she didn't come with us to the ghetto. She told you that she was going to camouflage herself as a Ukrainian girl when she learned that the Germans were recruiting a lot of them as laborers to be shipped to Germany. She could easily disguise herself as one—she was blond, with blue eyes, rosy cheeks, and a non-Semitic nose. She did go to Germany, where she worked as a maid for a German army officer's family. He was at the Eastern Front fighting the Russians, and she became a bonus, a free compensation benefit, a slave laborer. She was lucky—she took care of four children and the household. She wasn't hungry; she wasn't marked with the star of David; she even had a few hours free on Sundays. During those free hours she used to go to the outskirts of the city she lived in, with other young women maids, to look at the POW camp for French officers. Little by little she learned a few French words and befriended a young officer, bringing him stolen bread and cigarettes from the household where she worked. The over-the-fence romance between her and this young Frenchman continued until Allied forces liberated them at the end of 1944. The young officer took her to France, married her, and they went to Algeria, a French colony at the time, where he was a chief engineer of Gas de France, one of the biggest French industrial conglomerates. She lived in luxury in a beautiful villa, and had three Algerian housemaids—"slaves" of her own. Her new name was Madame Guilbert. Her husband's family belonged to aristocracy created by Napoleon Bonaparte, and his grandfather's name, Guilbert, was carved on the Arc de Triomphe in Paris. Clara converted to Catholicism to appease her husband's family and pacify them with this concession, since until then they considered their son's transgressions as a misalliance—a marriage between unsuitable persons.

After her husband retired on a rich pension, they settled in Lyon in a beautiful house, with a summer villa in the French

Alps. Clara's father, the Orthodox Jew from the little shtetl in Poland, would be turning over in is grave, lamenting the betrayal of his god. Too bad for him!

In 1960, by her invitation, I visited Clara in Lyon, visited her in-laws in Paris, saw her new name on the Arc de Triomphe in Paris, and spent some time in her villa in the French Alps. So everything I told you is true and not born of my imagination. But the part of this unusual and extraordinary story that I most wanted to tell you is one that honors you. Clara had two daughters. One she named Janine and the other one, Hélene—this shows her love for you: she named her daughters with the French versions of your two daughters' names.

This story always fascinated me by demonstrating the curious and unforeseeable interconnections between people. One amusing side of the story is that it may serve as a proof of a popular theory about "six degrees of separation." You and I were, because of Clara, separated from Napoleon Bonaparte by only "two degrees"—funny, ha?

◆　◆　◆　◆

I know, I know, my dearest, this letter turned into a long story, many little stories and images of you and me. All because I don't want to part from you . . .

◆　◆　◆　◆

One day, on a gray cloudy mid-morning after you and Janka had left for work, a cacophony of shouts in the German language awoke me from my half-dream state while I was still in bed. Through the window I heard *"Raus, raus, raus!"* The numbing, petrifying crescendo of screams was getting closer and closer to me. I heard heavy boots stomping on the stairs of our building, up and down, up and down; then I heard people being dragged out of the bedrooms in front of our room. The cries of the people who lived there, mixed with the German screams, were deafening.

I lay in the bed on my back, holding my bended knees with my arms in an awkward, clumsy position, hoping for this moment to pass. Suddenly, there was silence . . . and in this silence the door to our room opened and a Gestapo man with a rifle in his hand and a helmet on his head stood there in the frame of the door. The day was gloomy, and the room was poorly lit. He scanned the room and saw me! He moved his eyes around searching for more people, but instead fixed his eyes on the framed photograph of you and me; his gaze lasted only a few seconds but seemed to me forever. He then looked at me, and I knew instantly that he recognized me in this picture. His eyes moved again from my face to the photograph of you and me; when he heard the voices of Gestapo comrades approaching, he looked at me once again and put his forefinger to his lips in a universal gesture, ordering me to be silent. He then said to the other men in German something like, *"Keine Juden,"* meaning, "There are no more Jews here," and he walked out and closed the door.

What had just happened?! I knew it was unexpected, I knew I was not taken away with the other wailing people. Their mournful cries faded further and further from my ears. Silence, there was only silence . . .

The time from when the Gestapo man opened the door to its closing was probably less than a few seconds, but it was an eternity for me. My chance to live.

How many more chances would I get? Oh, how I longed for your embrace and the loving face of my big sister! Where were you? How will I explain to you what happened in this narrow, darkish ghetto room? What moved this man, who had his bestial, brutish duties to perform, to disobey his orders? I didn't know it then—and even now I don't have an answer. I want to believe that this man had seen, for a moment at least, an image of humanity in our photograph, a humanity that he had betrayed so many times, and this moment was his chance for redemption. Or maybe it was as simple as a father's love for his daughter? I don't know, but that is how I survived the beginning of the liquidation of the ghetto in the city of Lvov.

◆　◆　◆　◆

The night was dark and starless, and only faint light from the street lamp made eerie shadows in the room, when your whisper awoke me from my tired sleep. You rushed me to dress fast. I heard Janka telling you that the only safe place for us would be the hospital where she worked. We had to go there quickly under the cover of night. All three of us ran as fast as we could, you holding my hand in a trembling grasp, Janka leading the way. No word was even whispered. We passed several streets and entered the door of the hospital. Inside was a very long corridor, dimly lit, with black and white squares of tiled floor. The director of the hospital, Janka's boss, was waiting for us. He told you that the safest place for me would be the sick children's ward, and that he had a bed ready for me. You were to pretend, if anybody asked, that you were a worker in the hospital and he would vouch for that, although you didn't have the papers or documents to prove it. He was eager to help, but how wrong he was! His assumptions were no match for the heinous plans of the Nazis, which unfolded the very next day.

You sat by my bed in the roomful of sick children, some of them crying but most of them quiet or asleep. I told you everything that had happened to me during the day in the house we lived in. Again, you believed me! Why did you believe my story? A story that seemed unreal to me, but you knew that even a child's imagination couldn't make it up. You assured me that from now on you'd never leave me alone. Alas! How wrong you were!—your vow was also no match for the evil to come.

◆　◆　◆　◆

At dawn the next morning, clouds covered the blue of the sky. Several big trucks were positioned by the Gestapo in a row in front of the hospital and a squadron of Gestapo men unloaded themselves from the trucks and in very orderly fashion entered the hospital; some of them closed off the street so no one could escape. They looked like giant, armed lizards, their uniforms green with a bluish hue. The color of the uniforms was etched in my memory for many years, so much so that after the war and even until now every time I look at the pine trees called blue pine, that bluish hue reminds me of the scene of that morning. Those innocent pines I never touch and would never plant in my garden. Isn't it strange, Mama, what tricks our minds play with colors and smells? For the same reason, when being asked in this country for my "SS#," I always and invariably cross it off and write the full words "Social Security #." Once I even wrote a letter to a rock group popular in this country, asking them if they meant to write their name, KISS, with the same lightning bolts the SS men wore on their black uniforms.

All of the patients who could walk, adult and children, were loaded on the trucks for "relocation," as they were told. All those that worked in the hospital were lined up in the long black and white tiled corridor, at the end of which stood two SS men making a selection, ordering some to go to the left, some to the right door. The left door was to the big dining room of the hospital; the right door led to the trucks in front of the hospital.

Rumors spread by whispers toward the end of the line where we were standing—you holding my hand. The rumor was that "they" were taking away not only the sick but also those who didn't have a document called a *Kenkarte,* a special document given to everyone who worked in the ghetto. Seeing that the sick children were taken immediately to the lorries, you whisked me out of that sick children's room. You had promised never to leave me alone, and you held me close by your side.

You didn't have this now-required document—you didn't have it because you worked outside of the ghetto, on the "Aryan" side of the city, and only had a permit to leave the ghetto in the morning and to come back in the evening—and I saw the panic on your face. The face that I adored was pale, a visage of despair. The line was moving forward to the point of selection, where it divided into two branches—the left and the right. You had to make a decision, a desperate decision, a decision of love, a hero's decision . . .

◆　◆　◆　◆

My sweet, dearest Mama,

I'm sure you know the folktale of Solomon's wisdom in a case of two women who claimed the same baby. The story goes that Solomon proposed to settle the argument by cutting the baby in two with a sword, giving each woman half of the baby. At this point, the real mother of the child offered to surrender the baby, and the king, with psychological understanding of a mother's love, rendered the verdict in her favor. This folktale is one of the finest in the tradition of human wisdom. When the king's subjects heard of the judgment, they stood in awe of it.

◆　◆　◆　◆

As we were approaching the fork of the line, I heard your dramatic whisper in a half-begging, half-ordering tone, telling a woman standing next to us, "Take my child! Take my girl! And tell them she is yours!" And before pushing me toward her, you held my head in both of your hands, kissed me, and said, "Go! Go now!" The year was 1943. I was eleven years old, you were forty-seven, and this was the last time I saw you and felt the touch of your hands.

◆　◆　◆　◆

Remember the devil's pitchfork I drew for you? Your last destination was the extermination camp: Belzec, your last trip in this world. I always hoped that the love of your children sustained you and that your suffering was short, but there was no crowd to stand up in awe of your life and in honor of a mother's love.

Belzec. I have never seen it, but in my repetitive nightmares my eyes are fixed on a beautiful, intelligent, vital, noble woman—you—reduced to a name, Operation Reinhard, and belonging to the infamy of that time.

In three places, Belzec, Treblinka, and Sobibor, 1.7 million people were annihilated. It is incomprehensible to a normal human brain to conceive that an area smaller than nine hundred square feet could be a killing field to more than six hundred thousand innocent people, or could see the human cargo of one train transport eradicated, done away with, within no more than an hour.

✦ ✦ ✦ ✦

For many years after the war ended, every September I laid bundles of wild, red poppies in different places on Polish soil. I was saying goodbye to you.

It didn't matter where the flowers rested—the Polish soil was soaked with your blood.

Once again I part with you and all the tender memories of you.

✦ ✦ ✦ ✦

Goodbye Mama, my unforgettable Mama.

> Your daughter . . .
> Your daughter who
> Will always be part of you

In many uncountable ways you will always be part of her.

Letter to My Sister

* * * *

Dear Janeczka,

Janeczka was the name we used most frequently in the family when we talked to you or when we talked about you while you were away. This was our name of endearment for you; it instantly symbolized how precious you were to all of us: Mama, Papa, and me, your baby sister. Your official name was Janina (Yanina). Janka (Yanka) was a diminutive of that.

When you were born, in 1922, Mama was twenty-six years old, Papa was twenty-four, and I was not a biological entity yet, not for another ten years.

I know about the time of your appearance in the world from stories told to me by our parents.

Life was a little tough for the three of you, as often happens with young people just starting their life together. Within two years they had a precious baby to love and take care of. But they were young, energetic, and full of excitement and hope for their little family.

The difficulties came from the societal mores and customs, many of which they were breaking because the customs and mores were old and unjust. They believed, in their youthful idealistic way, that they could change them, if not in any other way than

just by example. The official laws and both their families' stag-
nant rules did not make it easy. Papa had just come from Vienna,
where he had had a year of apprenticing in a good clinic—we
would now call it an internship—and was applying for work in
Kulparkuw, a huge psychiatric hospital in the vicinity of Lvov.
While waiting and hoping for a positive answer, he took any physician's job available. Mama was taking care of her newborn baby
and could not work. They lived partially on money borrowed
from friends and eagerly waited to be independent.

Mama's closest family—her father, mother, one brother, and
two sisters—emigrated to Palestine the same year you were born,
and even if her parents had still been around, they probably would
have disowned her for daring to break with orthodoxy. Papa's parents were cold and distant, snobbishly disapproving of his choice
of a woman whom they considered below their class and status.
I'm sure you learned about all of this later in your life, but I'm recalling those events and just trying to imagine your time as a baby
and your childhood. You were growing up to be a city girl.

Now I can vividly see, as if in a film, their doting on you, and
their hearts warmed by every new thing you did. I remember a
story about you that Mama once told me. You were a growing,
healthy, and beautiful little girl, but no matter how they tried
with toys and songs and pictures in books to entice you to talk,
you wouldn't utter a word.

There was no "mama," no *"tata"* (Polish for *papa*); there was
no baby talk. They started to worry, and then in one surprising
moment when you were almost three years old, you decided to
break the silence, and full sentences with proper words, not baby
talk, started to flow from you, as if to show, "I'm ready, ready to
take on your world."

By the time you were about five years old, and Papa's dream
of obtaining a position hadn't materialized, they decided to leave
the big city so he could open a practice as a country doctor in the
provincial town of Warez.

From that time and until you were sent to school in Lvov, your daily life was probably not much different from mine when we lived there, except, as Mama told me, you didn't make friends easily. You didn't run with Gypsy kids or climb trees. You were contemplative, asked a lot of serious questions, and were very disappointed if they didn't have the answers. You were sent to the sophisticated big city of Lvov to attend school there, for the same reason I was supposed to go there just before the war started—you most likely would have outstripped the simplistic, provincial teachers in the town in which we lived.

◆　◆　◆　◆

My sweet, passionate, outspoken, intelligent, smart, and beautiful Janka, let me tell you what memories I have of you firsthand. You were supposed to be the longest-lasting witness of my life, and I, your little sister, who was supposed to see all of your dreams fulfilled.

◆　◆　◆　◆

You were my idol, but at the same time pangs of jealousy entered my childish mind when you were to come home for a short time during the school year, or for longer during summer vacation. My feelings were divided: I wanted to see you and be with you all of the time, but at the same time I was glad when your vacation with us was coming to an end. I don't think you were aware of this, except for my short outbursts of seemingly childish quips and jokes when I would say, "This is my Mama and Papa, not yours—go home!" All three of you would laugh and hug each other, teasing me that perhaps I was not the "real daughter." The psychological reasons for my feelings are clear to me now. All year round I was the center of attention, but upon your coming they needed, wanted, to shower you with their attention and love. My outbursts of envy were short and vanished completely when we spent time together, just the two of us, which was most of the time. In the evenings we gathered together in our "salon." You shared stories of school events and school friends with us, and Papa, if he was not called in to help some suffering souls in the villages, entertained us, playing beautiful piano pieces. It was heaven, and the memory of those moments are a balm, a balm that I still apply to my wounded mind.

◆　◆　◆　◆

You were beautiful, with your opalescent, iridescent black hair, shiny and straight with a slight wave around the forehead; it was shoulder length, and occasionally you would weave it into two thick, short braids. Your eyes were deep green, like big precious jewels, protected from the sun by long black lashes. You were tall and statuesque, even as a sixteen-year-old. Your face and gestures mirrored your moods, from pensiveness to irony to gaiety. You were perfect in my eyes. I could never understand why, as you often told me, you would trade all this richness and beauty for my straw-colored hair, my blue eyes, and the freckles that covered my nose and cheeks with the first burst of summer sunshine. You frequently kissed my nose and petted my cheeks with a quick swiping motion, as if stealing my freckles and placing them on your cheeks, saying, "See, I have them too!" Of course at that time neither one of us really cared how we looked; but today, my sweet big sister, I want you to know what my image of you was.

◆　◆　◆　◆

Now, at the beginning of the twenty-first century, science is beginning to unravel the mysteries of the brain. One of those mysteries is how long-term memories are stored and recalled. You would be fascinated by the new discoveries, as I am. But even if we still don't know exactly how memory works, one thing I know for certain is that it is one of the most magnificent and supreme endowments of our brain, for which I am eternally grateful to Mother Nature. At the end of the road I want to preserve all of my memories: the bad ones and the horrifying ones, the beautiful ones and the tender ones.

✦ ✦ ✦ ✦

It was a hot summer evening, the windows of our parents' bedroom were open, and a choir of birds was singing. We, all four of us—Mama, Papa, you, and I—were gathered together on their wide bed, and you were telling us about your life in school, about what you learned, about your teachers, about your visits to museums and theaters, about the rules you had to obey in school; you told us about your friends and even about some boyfriend who wrote to you secret letters about love and your beauty. We teased you about that, and you didn't mind it because you didn't like him that much—you liked another boy, who, to your disappointment, didn't write any letters to you and didn't pay that much attention to you. I felt pity for him; in no way, to my mind, could he find a better friend than you. That evening, I wasn't just a listener. I told you about my adventures and friends. The room was noisy and full of laughter and stories, and I remember you showed me the new steps you had learned of a dance called the waltz, which I clumsily followed. It was late at night when we finally dispersed, reluctantly, to our own bedrooms. That evening is not a static or stationary memory; it is a moving picture, like a film in color.

I loved being with you. You treated me as an equal, elevated my childhood to something higher, something important. You introduced me to the concept of god and gods as a way of easing some people's misery and explaining the unexplainable. As I remember it, you didn't mock those concepts; in your words they became tales from distant lands and people. Sometimes, late at night, you showed me stars from the balcony where Mama's oleanders bloomed; the stars had names. Some of them were planets. You showed me that I could see a rainbow not only in the sky after a rainy mist, but also in a crystal hanging from a fancy chandelier in our dining room. You told me that animals could think and feel love, hunger, and pain the same way we do. I already knew that from my Gypsy friends and from Bambi, but you made it more believable and more important. You told me that beyond this little city of Warez was the big city of Lvov, and beyond that was a big world, a whole world of different continents and people. You even told me that Mama and Papa were thinking about sending you to America to study in a university there after you graduated from *gymnasium*. Papa would pay a lot of money for the trip and for a permit for you to study there (10,000 zlotys, as I remember), and a friend of our parents, who lived there, would help you to establish yourself in this New World. This friend was a patient of Papa's. His life had been saved from a scourge of ravaging tuberculosis, and Mama had offered a place to stay in our home to recuperate. In the end, you didn't go to America; I think the parting would have been too hard to contemplate, and bad news about a possible war on the horizon was also a deterrent from separation. How painful it is to me to think about this decision now!

◆　◆　◆　◆

It is late, close to midnight, as I'm writing this letter to you. The summer is at its end, but here the air is warm, gentle, and calm. Through my open window, sitting at the desk, I see the full face of the moon, pale gold with wispy, grayish mares forming her eyes and mouth, looking the same way she did when we, as children, used to draw her face, Luna's face. The voices coming from the darkness of my garden are only those of cicadas making music with their delicate, transparent wings. I'm sure there is a good reason why they sing nature's song, but I selfishly take it as a gift for me, a gift that eases the flow of my thoughts about the times so long ago.

◆　◆　◆　◆

When we lived in Lvov, after escaping the German side of the divided country, we didn't spend much time together. You were a student at the university, studying to become a doctor, coming home late after courses and many hours at the library. I was in school too, and most of the time when you came back home, I was already asleep.

I remember one time I saw you acting as a "real doctor"—at least in my mind you were one, although you were just a first-year student in medical school. Mama became very sick; she suffered bad pains, couldn't eat, was in bed with a high fever, with drops of sweat on her forehead. Papa told us that she had a sick gall bladder and a stone that had formed in the pouch couldn't pass through. Her eyes were yellow and anything she ate would be expelled from her stomach. I had never before seen her sick, and it frightened me to see her lying in bed so helpless. Except for surgery, which she refused to have—a cause of tension between Papa and her—there was not much to be done but wait and hope it would resolve itself.

I saw you attending to her, giving her shots of morphine for pain, softly wiping her forehead with a wet cloth, giving and changing compresses on her stomach, spoon-feeding her some liquid nourishment or a wafer, or just sitting at her bedside and holding her hand. Yes, you definitely were a real doctor in my eyes. Famous painters depicted such scenes of a doctor attending the sick. I have seen them in different museums and books of art. In those paintings the doctor is always a man; in my memory painting it is you, a young, compassionate woman.

◆   ◆   ◆   ◆

On Sundays, you would sometimes take me to the movies or for a walk in the city, or you would take me to my ballet classes. When you had free time, you would stay there until the lesson ended and watch me do my pas and pirouettes, and on the way home you once told me that there are places in the world where girls could dream and fulfill those dreams, places where there were no wars and fears of the future, places where a girl like me could become a famous ballerina. There was a moment of silence between us, then we both burst in a spontaneous laugh and instead of walking somberly on the sidewalk, we joyously ran and hopped on the pavement like two kids with not a worry in the world.

You were my pal, my dream maker, and those were our secret times together.

As you know, none of our own family pictures survived the time of war in Poland. Even the Raphaelic picture of Mama and me, the one that saved my life in the narrow ghetto room, surely ended up in a heap of trash or a pile of ash. But in an eerie twist of circumstance, I brought a few pictures to America, and each of them had an image of you. The pictures had been saved by friends of our family who had the wisdom to escape from Eastern Poland. After the war, they gave them to Papa. I in turn gave them to my daughters in the hope they would keep them safely for the next generation. Most of them I gave to my older daughter, whose second name—here they call it "middle name"—is Janine in your honor.

◆ ◆ ◆ ◆

Those pictures, of course, are black and white or sometimes the color of sepia—reddish and brownish.

In one, there are three of us: Papa and you and I, walking on the street, dressed in warm coats, and each of us has a cap covering our heads. Another picture is of you and me sitting on the steps of the entrance to our beautiful house in Warez. Bambi, our terrier, is sitting proudly between us. One picture of you only is printed in the book that was sent to me from Israel by a friend of Papa's who emigrated there not long after I came to America. About this book, I must tell you later in this letter; it is devastating to me what is written there about the end of your life.

For now, my dearest, allow me the indulgence of looking at the photographic portrait standing on the shelf in my room: I look at a young and beautiful woman, with intelligent, sensitive eyes, with softness of expression, with a hint of an enigmatic or maybe even mystery-holding, *Gioconda*-like smile. She, our Mama, is holding on her lap a baby not much older than the age of two. The baby is embracing Mama's neck and holding her face tight, cheek to cheek with her loving protector. The baby is you. It seems as if Mama is protecting you from becoming an adult. Of course, I never knew you at this age, but I feel a peculiar, almost mystical kinship with Mama, and I, too, want to protect this baby—you—from all the dangers that might befall you.

That feeling, I'm sure, comes from the territory of my experience of motherhood. It comes from the esoteric, mysterious, and secret places of my psyche. I'm proud of it and cherish such soulful and stirring emotions.

Janka, my image of you will always be young. You will never have wrinkles or gray hair, you will never be feeble or crippled by aging. In my memory you'll always be beautiful, full of vitality and heroic deeds. This image will be my only compensation for the fact that we couldn't share our lives up to that old wrinkled age.

◆ ◆ ◆ ◆

You know the story of our life in the ghetto, so I'll not repeat it to you except to tell you that I knew of your clandestine activities there. Sometimes in the evening, when I was in bed pretending to be asleep, I would hear you and Mama talking in whispers about the secret contacts you had with people called "partisans" (here they call them "guerillas"), who were men from the "Aryan" side of town. You never mentioned their names, but you told Mama that you and those men were smuggling some arms into secret places in the ghetto to arm young Jewish men and women, and that soon you and your comrades would start fighting the Germans. During this fighting, a lot of people would be able to escape from the ghetto, disperse in the surrounding forests, and continue to engage in battles with the Germans from there.

Mama always asked you if you were sure you could trust those partisans, if you were sure that you would not be trapped by betrayal, delivered to the enemy by treachery that would mean a certain and cruel death.

You always answered sardonically, with a bitterness in your voice, that we all were marked for death and this was the only way you knew to live and at the same time preserve the dignity of your life. Mama was left at the end of those whispers begging you to be cautious and safe. Those nervous conversations always ended with both of you crying in each other's embrace. If by chance I gave the slightest sign of not being asleep, I heard you ask, your voice marked by nervous tension, "Helunia, are you awake?" I never answered. Somehow I knew it was dangerous to admit even to you what I overheard.

You know, as I recall all of this, I am convinced that Mama, like thousands of other people, never truly believed that the Germans' careful planning for the annihilation of millions could be carried out. She could never have accepted that a people that had produced and was proud of sharing with the world such giants of humanity and culture as Heine, Goethe, Schubert, Mendelssohn, and Mozart would turn en masse into "willing executioners." I was an ignorant child then, but now I would tell her that they also produced Wagner, whose hauntingly elevated and beautiful music was tainted by his poisonous and evil ideology, embraced by the Nazis.

◆　◆　◆　◆

So there I was, the only child in the dining room of the ghetto hospital, standing with a crowd of hospital workers, close to a woman, a stranger toward whom Mama pushed me just before they took her away from me forever. You never saw what happened. You were frantically running around the hospital looking for us. When you found me in this room, standing by a woman you knew as a nurse, she told you in a stenographic quickness what had happened just a few minutes earlier. You grabbed me in your arms, and as you held me tight the SS men loudly announced that all healthy people were to gather in front of the building until all the sick adults and children were packed in the huge trucks and moved away. Suddenly one of the SS men shouted and pointed at me with a gesture of his arm and high-pitched whistle, saying that I too should climb on the truck. Because of my age, it was clear to him that I wasn't a worker in the hospital, and the only alternative was that I was a patient, fated to go with the other children. All this was happening at lightning speed, but I remember you begging the director of the hospital, Doctor Litvak, to save me. He stepped out in front of the group of his people and told the shouting SS man that he vouched on his honor and his life that I was not a patient. The black-and-brown uniformed soldier of death, wearing a skull and crossbones on his cap, a symbol of his deadly mission, gestured that I could stay. It really didn't matter to him. He knew that in a few days we would all go to the same destination, but for now, he was in a hurry to fulfill his daily quota and get rid of the easiest prey—the sick.

What happened next is the worst I have ever seen of degenerated humanity. Whatever the philosophers may say, it proves to me the existence of absolute evil. The laws of relativity do not apply to these absolutes.

◆　◆　◆　◆

Small babies and sick children who couldn't walk were thrown out through windows from the fourth, fifth, and sixth floors, straight into the open trucks, their bodies and skulls smashing with the muted sound of a soft flap. I never heard their cries. I heard the cries of the women who tried to jump on the trucks in an attempt to catch the babies in midair, but they never made it—they were shot on the spot.

You covered my eyes with your hand, but it was too late. I cannot tell you what I was thinking at that moment, but I know that my psyche never lost the memory of what I saw, and deep ridges of sadness were carved there forever. I have had many repetitive nightmares throughout my sixty years since then—and this is one of them.

I dream of bodies flailing in the air, bodies of babies and children silently falling down, but in my nightmare they never reach the truck beds. I hold them suspended in the air by a magical power of my dream and let them flutter there, like butterflies or spiritual beings superior to humans, like mythological angels.

◆　◆　◆　◆

The tormented day was ending, and the evening was approaching. The trucks and the executioners were gone; the street in front of the hospital was empty. Rapidly you took me by my hand, and we ran up the stairs to the highest floor of the hospital building, breathing fast and stopping only for a second or two to catch a deeper breath. You found a small storage room, like a cell, with almost empty shelves around its walls, with a few towels and some yellow-stained pillows. Light was coming through a tall, very narrow window overlooking a big courtyard behind the hospital. You told me to stay there and be very quiet, not to answer or open the door. If anybody knocked on it or forced it open, I was to hide myself under the lowest shelf and cover myself with the pillows and towels. You told me you would be back as soon as darkness fell and take me to a safer place. You pressed me tightly in your arms and begged me again and again not to make any noise, saying that if I needed to go to the bathroom I should just do it in the corner of the floor and cover it with the rugs from the shelf. It all registered in my mind as you walked out of the cell, and I heard the key turning in the lock.

As I stood there alone, I felt I was at a turning point in my life. Death didn't mean that much to me from then on—just a passing from what "was" to nothingness. My only wish was for death to come fast with the least pain.

I moved slowly toward the window when I saw gray smoke rising toward the sky and a noxious smell sifted into the room through the window, left ajar. As the smoke was wafted here and there by the wind, it revealed piles of naked bodies, men and women, burning in the backyard of the hospital. The flames made the bodies contort and twist out of shape; it seemed as though some of them were still alive, with their mouths open and arms stretched to the skies. Those bodies I saw through the window, I realized, were patients so ill that they had been unable to walk to the trucks under their own power. The Germans' methodical plan of annihilation did not include any waste of time or energy: they burned the weakest right there and then.

◆　◆　◆　◆

My dearest, I never had a chance to tell you what I saw, I never had a chance to tell you that I didn't have tears in my eyes, that my newly acquired numbness protected me from becoming insane or screaming out loud. It wasn't numbness only; I had reached the limit when an eleven-year-old child's reality becomes surreal, when abnormality forces itself on normality and when forgetting is Mother Nature's only available mode of defense. Never mind that all I witnessed was stored in the darkest niches of my mind forever and would come back to haunt me again and again. In that past "present" time, I did not talk about it.

◆　◆　◆　◆

Dear Janka, let me stop for a moment from talking about this death- and horror-filled day. Allow me to distance myself for a moment—it is too dark there, too cold, and it's hard to come back to life after sinking into this fetid, black mud.

Let me tell you about Sparta. Sparta? you wonder. Why Sparta? More than two thousand years ago, when Sparta was at the peak of its power, this was one of their methods of preparing themselves for their victories. Shortly after birth, an infant was brought before the elders of the society, who decided whether it was to be reared; if the child was defective or weakly, it was disposed of. Until their seventh year, the children were educated at home. After that, their training was undertaken by the state. The training consisted, for the most part, of physical activity and fighting. Such subjects as music or literature occupied a very minor and subordinate position. By the time they reached the age of twenty, the children had become soldiers, servants of the state.

Yes, they were conquerors and subjugated many ancient city-states, including Athens. But there was never a Spartan Homer or Sophocles; there was never a Spartan Pythagoras, Aristotle, Euripides, Sappho, Solon, or Socrates. Spartans never climbed the Olympus of science, poetry, law, philosophy, or art.

◆　◆　◆　◆

The Germans of the Third Reich surpassed Spartan training. The Hitler Youth were trained not only in fighting but also, from early boyhood, in cruelty and the elimination of human compassion. I was told about boys in the Hitler Youth who were ordered to shoot their dogs—dogs they had raised from small puppies, loved and cared for, and for whom they had been allowed to develop a strong attachment. Those boys who shot their beloved companions were, by the age of twenty, the ones who threw sick babies from high windows and burned people too weak to walk to their deaths.

◆　◆　◆　◆

The Germans, if ever they had reached the Olympus of science, philosophy, poetry, and music, would have to climb it again, and with each step they would have to beg for forgiveness of those children thrown alive to their deaths.

I believe that children are not responsible for the sins of their fathers, but this idea applies only to the children who condemn not only the sins but the fathers as well. If we forgive and forget, as we humans repeatedly do, we insult our intelligence and hamper our ability to learn from our common history. I, for one, am not ready for dispensation of the sins I witnessed.

I'm sure that you would agree with me.

◆　◆　◆　◆

Now let me go back to this room where you left me on this never-ending day. I didn't have any urine or feces or even tears to expel from my body. The only physiological reflex was vomit, in response to the repugnant smell of burning human flesh and the image of it. The only thing my body was capable of doing was to vomit. My stomach expelled some undigested pieces of dark bread and a small amount of viscous fluid that was extremely bitter and sour. Minding your last words, I did it as noiselessly as I could in the corner of the room, covered the vomit with a rug, and sat on the floor next to it, in what I think was almost a state of stupor. I was conscious, but awareness and sensibility and perception were at their lowest ebb.

It was dark when I heard the key turn and you squeezed in through the slightly opened door. You couldn't see me sitting on the floor, but you called my name softly and I answered. You sat down close to me and handed me a small jar with milk and cooked potatoes. I'm sure you just brought me what you were able to procure for me, but it was perfect for neutralizing and absorbing the sour taste lingering in my mouth, and of course it was perfect to soothe my hunger too.

When I finished, you told me we must go. I was wearing a wrinkled skirt and blouse and shoes without socks. You brought for me a sweater that was a little too big and helped me put it on. We passed the empty stairs and corridors and walked out through the front door onto an empty street. The farther we walked away from the hospital, the darker the streets became. You obviously knew the way and destination. You also knew how to avoid the patrols of gendarmes and the Gestapo.

When the streets ended, we walked through an empty, grassy field to the bottom of the railroad embankment. This place was far away from the center of the ghetto and from the tunnel in the embankment, where not long ago, under the heavy guard of the Gestapo, we first entered this godforsaken place. After what was probably an hour or so of walking, we sat down on the ground. The night was so dark that I didn't even see your face so close to mine. You told me that we would wait for the sign of a soft whistle and birdlike chirping; when we heard it repeated three times, I was to run up on the embankment behind us, cross the rails, and run down on the other side toward the voice, giving the whistle and chirp as a password. There would be a woman waiting for me to take me to her home. You told me you couldn't go with me, but when the war ended, which would be very soon, you would know how to find me and we would be together again. You had to tell me that. How could you tell your baby sister that in one day she might lose two people who loved her the most, never to see them again? You couldn't expect me to understand or accept this unbelievable possibility. You told me to be brave and smart and not to cry, and, most important, to listen to this woman who would take me tonight and to always obey her, because she wanted the best for me. You told me she was a nurse in the hospital on the Aryan side of town, not in the ghetto, and her name was Jadwiga, but I was to call her Aunt Jadzia and to memorize the story she was going to teach me about her and me. I promised you all of this, shaking my head up and down in a gesture of understanding.

The sign of the whistle and the chirping bird came, in a triplet, and I ran over the railroad tracks, hearing only a few stones tumbling down, kicked by my feet.

I was gone, you were gone. This was the summer of 1943. After that night, I saw you only once, several months later, but I never again heard your voice or felt your touch.

The plans you and your comrades had to fight the Germans in the ghetto and facilitate the escape of many were never realized. The executioners' actions were well planned, and the Germans moved quickly toward their goal of exterminating people they judged not worthy of living.

My dear Janka, I know that you were aware of the devastation that had come upon us to this point, and that you were acutely aware of worse things to come, but you couldn't know all the cold numbers of killings.

That is why you, who were ready to give your life for the noble cause, deserve to know how right you were. I'm going to cite you some dates and numbers compiled much later, after the war ended, by the staff of the United States Holocaust Memorial Museum and published in the *Historical Atlas of the Holocaust*:

Encouraged by German forces, Ukrainian nationalists staged violent pogroms against the Jews in July 1941, killing about 4,000 Jews; another "pogrom," known as the Petlura Days, was organized in late July [Symon Petlura was a Ukrainian who organized pogroms after World War I].

For three days Ukrainians went on a rampage through the Jewish district of Lvov—they took groups of Jews to the Jewish cemetery and to Lunechi Prison and shot them—2,000 people were killed and thousands more were injured. . . .

In early November 1941, Germans established a ghetto in the north of Lvov. Thousands of elderly and sick were killed as they crossed the bridge on their way to the ghetto. . . .

In March of 1942, Germans began deporting Jews from the ghetto to Belzec killing center; by August of 1942, more than 65,000 were deported and killed. Thousands of Jews were sent to forced labor to the nearby Janowska Camp. The ghetto was finally destroyed . . . in early June 1943. The remaining ghetto residents were sent to Janowska labor camp or to Belzec. Thousands of Jews were killed in the ghetto during this liquidation.

These excerpts give the cold facts in a short few sentences. But my letter to you has another purpose. I want you to know how I saw these facts as a child, how immense and inexplicable everyday suffering was, and how hard it is for me even to find words to describe it. I want you to know that my desire to describe those times is at least twofold: first, that my voice, meek and as inadequate as it is, might humbly represent all those voices that were silenced by self-appointed torturers and executioners; and second, that my grandchildren and their children, when they read in school history books about these times, will also know that behind those "cold facts and statistics" were thousands of mothers like ours, sisters like you, and children like me who had their souls and hearts and feelings shattered and smashed into ashes, with only a few left to tell the story of all-encompassing darkness.

◆　◆　◆　◆

After I had stayed a few days in her house, "Aunt Jadzia"—the woman who picked me up on the other side of the railroad—invited into her house a relative to take care of her two children, a six-year-old boy, Voytek, and his five-year-old sister, Magda, while she was out of town for a few days to attend to some urgent matter. She told this woman, whose name was Pani Wanda, Mrs. Wanda, that I was a niece of her husband's and, being an older girl, was there also to help in the household.

Pani Wanda was an older woman, short and skinny, with short, salt-and-pepper hair, a square, wrinkled face, deep-set eyes, and a hoarse, almost manly, voice. She was a devout Catholic, and before going to bed every evening and on rising in the morning she knelt in front of a picture of the Virgin Mary that she had brought with her and prayed loudly, holding in her hands a rosary and moving her clawlike fingers from one bead to another as she said one Hail Mary after another. She made all three of us children do the same. She was unpleasantly surprised that I didn't know the prayers, while the two younger ones did. She started questioning me as to my kinship to the hostess, and from my confused and incomplete answers she realized that I was a Jewish girl who was hiding in this house. She didn't approve of Aunt Jadzia hiding lousy, mangy Jews, as she eagerly told me, and a couple of days later she made it clear to me why. She had learned about an important event to take place, and she wanted all of us to see it. "They are going to burn the Jews in the ghetto," she said, "and tonight we are going to watch it." We made our way there in the evening. By the time we got to the edge of the ghetto, it was almost dark. As we climbed the railroad embankment—the same one I had climbed just a few days earlier to escape from the ghetto, but much farther from the city—the sky was illuminated by high, red flames. Some flames were smaller, visible at different points; then they merged into one immense inferno. There was a crowd of people standing tightly together, watching this spectacle without horror or tears on their faces. The woman who brought us here turned to me and, pointing with her stretched arm to the flames, directed her voice toward me and said in a husky, ominous voice words I will never forget."You watch and remember," she said, "that burning your people is the right and just thing to do because you killed our Lord Jesus Christ, and then you Jews killed Christian babies to make matzohs with their blood in it. This killing fire is the only glorious and good thing the Germans are doing. This way you'll cease to exist." And she finished the speech with the sacred word, "Amen!"

I remember the words exactly as she said them because I heard them many times later in my life, even after the war. This woman stood at this surreal setting of hell's fire, the devilish realm, the place of torment and destruction, with her eyes mirroring the flames and full of hate. She was the personification of the ugly old witch from my scary book of fairy tales. I was waiting to see if, any moment now, she would fly away into the skies over the fires and smoke, away from me. But she didn't, she came home with us. To the credit of my childish mind, I never believed a word she said, and if I had known how to do it, I would have laughed at her disdainfully. This woman's words, however, succeeded in teaching me that from now on many people would hate me for reasons not understandable to me and would prove this hate in more ways than I knew existed.

My mind was occupied with more important thoughts—thoughts of you, my sister. It was too frightening to me even to imagine that you might be there, in that infernal abyss. I repeated to myself over and over again your promise that we would see each other again. And we did!

It was a few months later, at the beginning of winter, when I was wandering the streets, lonely, homeless, hungry, and cold. The day was gray, the sidewalks covered with a slush of partly melted snow, which had fallen that year earlier than usual. The street's name was Lyczakowska. It ran up the hill, where it dead-ended at the top by the large buildings of a psychiatric hospital, commonly known as Lyczakow. If people wanted to offend someone or say he was stupid or crazy, they instead said, "He is a runaway from Lyczakow." But for me at that time, it was a good place; I accidentally learned that in the afternoon the gate to the hospital was open, and I could sneak in behind the kitchen building and find some scraps of food in the trash bin. Mostly there were pieces of potatoes or beets, but if I was lucky I would find some chicken bones with remnants of meat on them. Sometimes the kitchen workers would shoo me away from the bin as they would shoo a stray dog, but I would come back the next day for the same reason a stray dog would—hunger.

I was walking up to that place on what I considered the safe side of the sidewalk, the side closest to the buildings. It was safe because if I saw somebody who wanted to chase me, which happened often, I would have a chance to dash into the nearest building, run up the stairs, and hide. This time, however, there was no danger, just an unexpected joyous surprise: from far away, I saw you, my Janeczka, my sister, coming toward me on the "unsafe" side of the sidewalk. You wore Mama's old winter coat, which still looked elegant with its remnant of a red fox fur collar, and your head was covered with a brown, wooly kerchief. You noticed me just as I saw you. I made a move with outstretched arms, ready to run toward you, but you made a secretive gesture to me to stop and not to approach you. I noticed that you were carrying a big, soft traveling bag. Instinctively, we both slowed down our paces so we could see each other for a little while longer. We passed each other in silence, and only our eyes and faint smiles of recognition said everything it was possible to say. I turned my head back to see you once more as you sped up your walk. Our contact lasted no more than two or three minutes, but in my still childish naïveté this encounter was a confirmation of your promise that we would see each other again.

We didn't. This would be the last time.

Knowing what I know now, on that day, you were probably carrying important things for the underground in that big bag and couldn't jeopardize your work, your fellow fighters, the cause, yourself, and me.

What I also know now (from the *Historical Atlas of the Holocaust*) is that after the liquidation and burning of the ghetto, you and the others still strong enough to work were relocated to Janowski labor camp. This camp, as we now know,

was set up in 1941 and was owned and operated by the SS and called German Armament Works, where Jews were used as forced labor in carpentry and metalwork. It was also a transit camp in the mass deportation of Polish Jews to the killing centers in 1942. Jews underwent a selection process in Janowska similar to that used at Auschwitz-Birkenau and Majdanek.

Those classified as fit to work remained at the camp for forced labor. The majority unfit for work were deported to Belzec and killed or were shot at the Piaski (Sandy) Ravine. In the summer and fall of 1942, thousands of Jews from the Lvov ghetto were killed there. In November 1943 the prisoners were forced to open the mass graves and burn the bodies as Germans attempted to destroy the traces of mass murder of "Aktion 1005." As the documents presented at the Nuremberg Trial showed, "In the same November 1943, these prisoners staged an uprising and an attempt of mass escape. A few succeeded, but most were recaptured and killed."

But I'm getting ahead of myself. I'm quoting all those official data for you in a fervent desire to let you know that the history of those times, the history of you, is not forgotten. I keep imagining that maybe if you had lived centuries ago, a dramatic saga would be written about you; you would have become a folk heroine with a statue of your likeness erected in some mystic forest.

In late autumn of 1944, when the Russians reoccupied Lvov and pushed the Germans westward, I was still roaming the streets of the city, still lonely and hungry, but this time without the ever-present fear of being hunted for killing. I was endlessly looking to find you before I was told that you had probably perished. I heard that all Jews who survived had put their names on pieces of paper and nailed them on the wall of a burned synagogue that stood in the center of the city. I tacked my name to this wall in the hope that you would find it. I sometimes would stop women walking on the street, women of your height and black hair, pull them by the sleeves of their clothes and force them to look at me, hoping that I would see your face. But it never was; it was always the face of a stranger. For many years after the war ended, until my late teens, bouts of guilt descended on me like dark clouds. Why was I here? Why were you gone? You already had shown what it meant to be human; I had yet to prove myself.

When I decided to become a physician, a healer of body and soul, the kind I imagined you would have been, that cruel fate never allowed you to become, I tried my best, and my hope is that I didn't disappoint you.

◆　◆　◆　◆

For many years after the war, after Papa and I were reunited, we didn't know what had happened to you, where and how you died, and sometimes we even had a fleeting, wispy hope that we would find you. We heard of people and families suddenly reuniting after being blown into different parts of the world by almost incredible circumstances and by the turmoil of the war. One day Papa decided to travel to a southwestern city of Poland, Wroclaw, where most of the Poles from Lvov had resettled after the Yalta Conference of February 1945 had once again shuffled the borders of Poland. Wroclaw had been the German city of Breslau before the war, while after the war Lvov became Lviv, a city belonging to Soviet Ukraine. The Germans were defeated, the Ukrainians bet on the wrong horse, and Poland became a satellite of Soviet Russia.

Papa was counting on finding people from Lvov who would know what happened to you. He did, but they did not tell him the whole truth. Papa learned from a man who had been one of the partisans in the Lvov area that he had met and known you as a member of a different group of fighters, hiding in the forests surrounding the city. He knew that you had belonged to a group of partisans code-named Ivan Franko, and that you had participated in many actions against Germans. You died in one such action, an attempt to blow up a railroad bridge. Destroying it would have crippled the essential transportation of German arms and soldiers to the Eastern Front. He also knew that you had been active in buying arms from German soldiers who stole them from their own army and carried them to secret hiding places. As a woman, the only woman in your group, you were less conspicuous, and it was safer to give you this task to perform.

It is known that those clandestine assignments were given frequently to women or children. I now assume that when I saw you on Lyczakowska Street with a big bag in your hand, you were on one of your dangerous, secret missions.

Remember the book I told you about, which was written and published in Israel in 1979, thirty-six years after your death, and sent to me in America as a gift? One chapter in this book is dedicated to you and describes in detail, supported by documents preserved in the archives of the Nuremberg trials of the Nazis, what really happened on the day you perished. The document is a report by General Katzman, the SS chief in the district of Galicia, to his superior, SS Polizei Führer Krüger in Krakow. The report describes the episode and how it was dealt with. The book is written in Hebrew, and the chapter about you was translated for me by a physician friend here in the United States.

And here is the story:

Two drivers, supposedly Ukrainians working for the Germans, who previously had been known to sell arms and ammunitions to undercover partisan groups, this time agreed for 20,000 zlotys to transport two dozen people, ammunition, and explosives to the area of Brody (a small town near Lvov), where you and your group were to arrange the placement of explosives along a stretch of railroad tracks and under a bridge, both strategic to the Germans for transporting armed forces to the battlefields. After driving for some time in the darkness of night, both drivers suddenly stopped. In a few moments it was clear that they had betrayed you and had driven you to a Gestapo station instead. A brief firefight between your people and the Germans ensued—a fight doomed to failure by the simple fact of surprise and the overwhelming manpower of your enemies. All of your comrades were killed on the spot, but you and a fellow combatant, also a woman, were captured alive and taken to Gestapo command headquarters in Lvov. Your friend was tortured and then hanged in the streets of Lvov as a gruesome warning. You expired in agony from repeated, sadistic tortures inflicted on you in the dungeons of the Gestapo.

At the end of this chapter about you I read this sentence: "The beloved, good-hearted Janka lost her soul in the cellars of the Gestapo. With honor and glory, blessed be her shining memory!" Indeed!

A warm feeling overcomes me that this is how you'll be remembered by strangers, but I, your sister, am unable ever to overcome my sadness, grief, and sorrow over losing you and over how unjust and cruel were your life's last moments.

Marko Strauss, the author of the book, inscribed the opening page: "To Helena, the sister of the heroine in my book—for safekeeping and lasting memory—M. S."

◆　◆　◆　◆

After the war, in Warsaw, where I lived, a statue was erected to commemorate the uprising in the Warsaw ghetto and the subsequent annihilation of its Jewish population. I visited it frequently, alone, looking at the figures and faces, carved in high relief, of heroes and martyrs of the infamous times. In my imagination, some of the faces symbolically represented you and Mama and created a palpable closeness between us.

◆　◆　◆　◆

When I graduated from medical school, it was customary that along with a diploma, a Hippocratic Oath printed in fancy letters on vellum was given to each of us during the graduation ceremony. One day, when I was again flooded by the memory of you, I rolled up this parchment, tied a green ribbon around it, and jumped into an electric tram, which landed me close to the statue of the ghetto heroes. I placed the Hippocratic Oath at the base, and I remember I smiled. I was happy to evoke good memories with this symbolic gift to you. I was saying good-bye to you.

◆　◆　◆　◆

In my world even now the dead are not dead.

Janka, I will remember you with tenderness and love until memory is no more.

Your sister

Letter to My Father

• ◆ ◆ ◆

Dear Papa,

A couple of days ago I reread my diary, written when I was eighteen and had just graduated from high school. Some of the words and entries are naïve; some reflect ideology that was not my own, but was prevalent among the youth of that time; some describe my friendships and romances, relationships typical for a teenager anywhere in the world that now bring a smile to my aging face. Some descriptions of nature, beautiful summer evenings, walks on the shores of the Baltic Sea and on the banks of the Vistula River are written with the sensitivity of youth, and although they are written in a language I don't use anymore, a language whose sound and structure seem strange to me now, those descriptions, my humility aside, show perhaps a small spark of talent in an eighteen-year-old girl. I left those diaries with my friend in Poland for safekeeping, and she sent them to me a few years ago, sensing that her life was coming to an end. You knew her: she and I worked in the same hospital in Warsaw for many years, the same one where you were the chief of the internal medicine ward. Her name was Jagusia, short for Jadwiga. She was born in the same year as our Janeczka, and I "adopted" her as a substitute older sister.

The real reason I am writing to you about my diary is an entry written by me on January 27, 1952, about ten years after all my experiences of wartime took place. On that date, I admit that I never told you all the details of my life under Nazi occupation. I told you the facts, yes, that Mama was dead, Janka was dead, your whole family was dead. I told you in "shorthand" how it happened, but never the actual details. In this diary, which you never read, I permit myself to admit how painful it would be to recount all those events, but at the same time I state with insightful intuition the benefit to my psyche such catharsis could bring. Of course, I didn't say it in such fancy words; I simply said that if I could free myself of those memories by telling them, by describing them, my nightmares might stop and the pain might stop and I might feel some relief. But I never did tell my story, not until now, more than half a century later. Even after I moved to America, it was too painful. I remember one evening in the early 1970s, I was watching with my children a movie shown on television about life in the ghetto in Poland. I started to cry inconsolably, and when my children were startled and surprised by my sudden outburst, the only thing I could say was, "That's how it was! It was a really bad time!" I felt it would be selfish of me to bring forth to them the cruelty of my experiences.

I don't feel that way anymore.

◆   ◆   ◆   ◆

Just before you found me, Papa, in the autumn of 1944, I was taken in by a woman who saw me putting my name on the wall of a ruined synagogue in Lvov. The woman's name was Dr. Lieberman. She was a dentist who knew you before the war and recognized the name. When she learned that I was alone, she told me to put her address on this piece of paper on the wall, because I would be living with her now. She said it as a matter of fact, and I agreed to her offer. It would be a better idea than being alone again. She never told me how she had survived, but when the

Russians came to Lvov and she came out of hiding, she rented an apartment in the middle of the city and opened her practice.

It remained a mystery to me how she got the money, although I suspect she paid her way with jewelry and gold she had somehow stashed away before the war, and those valuable resources helped her to survive. I know of other cases where having gold coins or jewelry, in conjunction with the greed of some "noble savior" Poles, helped some Jews to survive, sometimes until the end of the war. But more often than not they survived for just a few days, to be betrayed when the shiny funds ended. In this overwhelmingly Christian country, Judas was a prominent figure.

During the several weeks I stayed with the lady dentist, I had a warm house to live in and, although the food was simple, I was not hungry. At age twelve, I became her assistant; she taught me how to sterilize her instruments, and I even learned how to mix silver fillings for the teeth of her patients. She paid me a few groszy, a few pennies, so I could buy some apples or pears in the street market, which always gave me a feeling of abundant luxury.

As I recall, I wore clothes that were too big for me and shoes that were also too large, but neither had holes—so this was luxury as well.

The only luxury that I truly desired at that time was to have somebody to love me, to embrace me, to tell me that I was important, and to make sure that what had happened would never happen again. Would I ever have it?

◆　◆　◆　◆

One day, into this makeshift combination apartment/dental office walked a young woman who asked for me by name. She was a good-looking, robust woman who spoke only in Russian and Ukrainian. It is a curious thing that I have forgotten her name, because the news she brought with her was so overwhelming.

She told us that she came from Russia, that she was a nurse in a Russian military hospital where you worked as a doctor, and that she knew you well. She told us that she had a family in Kiev, the capital of Ukraine, and that she had gotten permission from the military authorities to travel from the depths of Russian territory to visit her family. She also told us that you had learned about her trip and given her money to make an additional trip from Kiev to Lvov to look for your family. By word of mouth, she found my name and address on the walls of the ruined synagogue. She told us that she was authorized by you to arrange, for whomever of your family had survived the war, a trip to Russia, to the place you were living. Well, her task turned out to be easy—I was the only one alive.

The story she told us on that day would be nearly impossible to invent, but still, it was so unbelievable that the lady dentist, my protector at the time, demanded of the young woman some proof of the verity of her words. She said she would bring the proof the next day.

What she brought the next day were five letters from you: one to your parents, one to your brothers, one to Mama, one to Janka, and one to me. All the letters were handwritten on yellowish, lined paper with purple-colored ink. I read them all. In all of them there was a choice for the recipients of those letters: to make the trip to Russia or to wait until the end of the war when you hoped to come back. The letter to me was written in clear cursive, so any child could read it easily; and to prove to me that you really were my Papa who was writing it, you mentioned happenings from my childhood that only you and I could know, begging me to believe your identity. At the end of the letter you promised me, when I came to you, to make my life sweet and beautiful again for always.

No other words could have made me more happy; even if all this might in the end turn out to be a big lie, such a fairytale ending is all I wanted and desperately needed to hear. Dear Papa, you also wrote that the woman who was to give me the letter would travel with me back to you; that I was to listen to her and always be near her; that I must not get lost in the crowded trains. You gave me instructions that during the trip I should keep myself as clean as possible and never drink unboiled water or milk; the nurse also knew to give me only well-cooked food. All those precautions were necessary to avoid getting ill with the typhoid fever rampant in the land I would be passing through. It was agreed that in two or three days, after procuring for me a permit and ticket to travel, your emissary, the Ukrainian nurse, would come. When she came, I was ready: bathed and clean, with hair trimmed just above my neck, dressed in a woolen skirt and sweater and laced-up shoes reaching my ankles. My luggage was simple: I had a bag sewn from a piece of a blanket of a dark green and grayish color; in it I had a single sweater, a woolen cap and mittens, a small white rag in which a piece of dark brown soap was hidden. The nurse added a few other things to my bag: a half-loaf of bread, a small bag with sugar cubes, a big metal drinking cup, and a small gadget that turned out to be not only very useful during our trip, but also created a real sensation among the mobs of Russian peasants traveling with us and made me, when I used it, a center of attention. This gadget was a rectangular metal box about four and a half inches wide and three and a half inches thick. The top of the box was cut in the middle, so it could be opened to a forty-five-degree angle to the sides in such a way that it created a base for a cup to be placed on it. In the middle of the box's bottom, I would place small squares of grayish, slightly opalescent tablets, of which three dozen came with the box. The tablet was then lit by a match, and the whole contraption became a miniature oven on which I could, in my cup, boil water or milk or the thin soup that was sold in some rail stations on our way.

Her brother, as my companion nurse told me, had stolen this box from the backpack of a dead German soldier. Forgive me for such a long digression from my main story, but it struck me as eerie how this little device, which opened such a flood of possibilities, had passed from hand to hand in the course of its inanimate existence, ending up in my hands for my comfort. This little metal box traveled with me from Lvov to Penza, deep into Russia, came back with me to Warsaw, Poland, and then accompanied me to America. I finally lost it here but obviously did not forget the train of thoughts it generated.

◆　◆　◆　◆

Our trip from Lvov to Penza, the city where you lived, lasted nine days! During those nine days, we covered a distance of slightly more than 1,600 kilometers (about 1,000 miles), which today would take probably no more than two hours by plane. The train was stopped many times, for hours and sometimes for a day or two, in big cities and in godforsaken little train stations in the middle of nowhere. It was held up or put on side rails to give way to endless trains with soldiers and supplies going in the opposite direction—to the West. The train cars were filled with masses of people displaced by war—men, women, and children trying to get to their homes or to relatives. Many of them had been expelled or forced to flee their native land by the movements of the German or Russian armies. They were sitting on benches, on the floors, in the doors, and some even on the steps of the train entrance.

Food was hard to come by, but my nurse protector had her entrepreneurial ways. Helped by your money and her knowledge of both Ukrainian and Russian, we were able at some stations to get some food—bread, milk, even soups and eggs on occasion. She never left me alone in the train for fear of losing me, so we were always together on our escapades out of the train and our hunts for food. Surprisingly, more food was available around those small unknown country stations than in the stations in big cities such as Kiev, Kharkov, and Voronezh, which had almost none.

I had my first lessons in the Russian language on this train. I learned the name of foods and simple words, like *spasibo* for "thank you," and *do svidanja* for "good-bye." It was easy for me because I knew a close relative of the Russian language—Ukrainian. I even learned that I was *krasivaja dievochka*, a pretty girl, a compliment given to children so frequently in peaceful times, long ago forgotten by me. The air was cold, with sad, gray skies, crying with rains on and off. Even the sun was tired, and when it showed its face occasionally, it dispensed very little warmth. At night, the train was dark with a flicker of candlelight here and there. Sometimes a mother's lullaby to soothe her child would break the silence. And in this time between the dusk and dawn she would be joined by a chorus of sad folk songs, divided like an echo of high and low tones. It was a music I learned to love. It was different from the music that you played on piano, but it suited me better in this time on the train. It met my need for calm. It was perfect.

Despite external circumstances, I was happy in a way I had not been for a long time. This state of my mind brought to me the images of you and me of long ago.

◆   ◆   ◆   ◆

I began to recall what I knew about you: how you looked, how you worked, what your passions were, and what we did together. You were taller than Mama by at least a head. Your head was bald on the top, and you shaved the remnants of gray hair growing around the bottom of your skull as soon as they showed up; you had blue eyes that seemed very big, magnified by the lenses of the eyeglasses you wore. You had a nice, bouncy way of walking and your hands had long supple fingers. You knew many languages: the ancient Hebrew taught to you by your grandparents, then the German you learned in the school you attended when Galicia and Lvov were part of the Austro-Hungarian Empire under Kaiser Franz-Joseph. You knew the Czech language from the time you studied medicine in Prague. You had studied abroad because admission to medical schools in free Poland was limited to minority students, and particularly Jews, by the unwritten principles of *numerus clausus* or *numerus nullus*. You learned French as an admirer of their superb literature, Ukrainian because the majority of your patients in Warez were Ukrainians. You ended up as a country doctor there because, as a Jew, you were refused a position in a psychiatric hospital in Lvov. Psychiatry was your passion, probably fueled by Freudian psychoanalysis. You continued as a matter of principle to reapply for that position yearly for more than ten years, but although the position was still open, you never got approval. This became the subject of satirical jokes in our family. In the end, the joke was on those who refused you; you wouldn't have gone there even if they had accepted you. You made exceptionally good money for those times, as you told me later, 5,000 zlotys per month or more. It didn't come easily to you. You worked hard, and not only in your office: you were available to your patients day and night. If a woman in a surrounding village was about to have a baby, if somebody couldn't breathe because of pneumonia or galloping tuberculosis, if somebody was dying of a ruptured appendix, or broke his leg working in the field, they would send their horse-drawn buggies to bring you to the rescue and to heal them. If death came to them, you closed their eyes and consoled the families. If they couldn't pay for your efforts, you treated them equally with the rich ones. The poor ones would bring payment as they could, some chicken or eggs or potatoes to Mama as a gesture of gratitude. Those simple people adored you. It was always a mystery to me how could they turn against you and your family after so many years of your kindness and hard labor.

I remember one beautiful summer day when I witnessed an outpouring of respect and love to you. On that day, word came that you were coming back to our little town after more than a month away. The road to town was lined with peasants and town dwellers to greet you, and little children, many of whom you had helped to bring into this world, were throwing flowers in front of the car, a luxurious automobile in which you were sitting together with Count Hulimka. Count Hulimka was an aristocrat, a rich landowner in this part of the country, who, along with his mother, was your patient for many years.

What happened? Why this triumphal comeback? Why in the count's luxurious Hispano-Suiza, with him sitting next to you? Allow me, my dear Papa, to retell to you this story. The story, to be understood, has to start like any good story, from its beginning.

In those prewar days, you were a sympathizer with the Communist movement in Poland, as were many members of the intelligentsia at that time, especially Jewish intellectuals and those for whom this ideology was a promise and the only way to apply the ideas of *liberté, egalité, et fraternité*. How wrong all of you were, history would shortly prove. It would prove how noble ideas could turn barbarous and mercilessly cruel for millions in the hands of all sorts of tyrants. Only toward the end of your life did you finally admit to yourself how colossal the mistake was. For many years this mirage, this deceptive reality, was your life. It is difficult to admit to a wasted life and a wasted idea.

But returning to that summer day: Mama was holding my hand as we stood with a crowd of people in the town's square; we were there when you got out of the automobile, picked me up, and held me tightly in your arms. On that day you returned from jail, held there accused of helping and aiding a group of your friends who were members of the Polish Communist Party; many of them, after a short trial, ended up in an infamous jail called Bereza Kartuska and spent many tortured years there. Instrumental in your release was your friend and patient, Count Hulimka, who testified on your behalf.

◆　◆　◆　◆

Because of your constant work, there were not too many moments that we had together, only the two of us. Mostly, during late evening suppers, we were all together, especially during the precious times when Janka was with us on vacations from school. I remember, however, some of those "you and I" moments.

On winter nights before we all retired, Handzia, our house-maid and cook, would start a fire in each bedroom in those beautiful, tall, tiled fireplaces. My bedroom had dark green tiles, and the furnace was framed with tiles depicting *agavic*, flybane mushrooms, called *muchomory* in Polish, red with white polka-dots, with gnomes sitting on them with red-painted caps, big noses, and big smiles. In real nature, those mushrooms with red heads and white polka dots were in fact deadly poisonous, but in children's fairy tales they were inhabited by sweet little gnomes, *krasnoludek* in Polish, who made children's wishes come true. On those cold winter nights, you would come to my bedroom to kiss me good night. If the room were still not warmed up, you would hold my blanket close to the furnace to warm it for me, then cover my body with an envelope of warmth, sit on the edge of my bed, and tell me sweet good-night stories.

Those were magic times when my evening reality would cross the border to dreamland. I regret that I don't remember my dreams, but I'm sure they were heavenly. Sometimes in the summers or in springtime, flavored with the aroma of blooming lilacs and jasmines, you would take me along on your visiting tours of your patients. While waiting for you, I would play with the children, who became my companions in exuberant, child-ish, foolish plays. One time, so memorable for me, in a household where you visited your patient a cow was about to give birth to a calf. But something went wrong, and the man of the household came running to you, begging for your help in this delivery. All the children and I ran to the barn, and cuddled in the corner with eyes wide open in amazement. We saw a cow standing on the straw-covered floor with nearly half of the baby cow hanging out under her tail. The cow's stomach was heaving in rhythmic spasms, trying to push her baby out, her long tail flailing rapidly from side to side. I remember that you put long rubber gloves on your hands and with intense effort helped the baby cow to come out. The baby cow fell on the thick layer of straw, and you cleaned her pink nose and mouth, which were covered with a gluey, thick substance. When the calf took its first breath, the mama cow turned her head toward her baby and with a thick pink tongue started to clean it off. For me, it was a spectacle to be remembered, and, as you see, I still do. On the way home I was full of excitement and emotion about what I had just witnessed. I remember you told me that human babies are born pretty much the same way. This biology lesson you were trying to teach me that day was too much to register in my mind, but when I was a twenty-five-year-old intern in an obstetric ward and for the first time in my life saw a baby born, and saw the mother move from pain to tears of joy when holding the newborn in her arms, I cried with her, perceiving at last the commonality of nature's laws.

We made occasional trips to the big city of Lvov, a place of city pleasures and treats, but for one reason or another the countryside fascinated me more.

On a few occasions you also took me with you on your visits to the Countess Hulimka's manor. She was a widow, and her only son rarely stayed there with her, spending most of his life in Paris and traveling all over Europe in the luxury their estate provided. As a child I didn't blame him for not staying with her; I thought he was as scared of her as I was. She was a tall, ugly, skinny woman with a long face, protruding teeth, and a stiff posture. They owned thousands of acres of rich agricultural land worked by peasants. The palace they lived in was huge, surrounded by beautiful gardens and trees. Her husband had died many years before, and it was rumored that many children in the surrounding villages—part of the estate—were his, born to young and beautiful Ukrainian girls. The old countess ruled the estate with iron will. She was hoping that her son would one day bring a highborn wife from Europe, but he never did. When she received her peasants, she stood on the wide terrace of the palace and by feudalist custom they kissed her hand while kneeling before her. When the audience was finished, the peasant men and women backed away facing her and moved that way for some distance, daring to turn their backs to her only from far away.

No wonder I was afraid of her. The reason for you taking me there was not, of course, to meet the countess or her son. The reason was much more important and exhilarating to me. They had an animal farm: not just ordinary animals I could see in any peasant's household, but also sables, red foxes, and silver foxes, deer, and even a couple of bears. All those animals were caged, but when they had babies, usually in spring or early summer, the keeper would allow me to hold those babies in my arms or on my lap, and feed them, pet them, and talk to them. For some reason I got attached to one little baby fox. I even gave him a name, *czarnulek,* an endearment from *czarny,* meaning "black." He was a black fluffy cub, with shiny brown eyes, a long pink tongue, and needle-sharp, snowy white teeth. I was convinced that he loved me and wanted to be with me. I didn't care that he would grow into a big silver fox. I visited him two or three times, crying when we parted. You promised to buy him for me, I'm sure just to avoid my begging, but it never happened. I held it against you for a long time. This was my first lesson, of many to come, in broken promises.

◆　◆　◆　◆

The crowded train, full of strangers, was going through the steppes of the Ukraine, through dry, grassy lands and villages ravaged by war. As we slowly entered the land of Russia, my memories of my happy childhood began fade as I recalled the fearful existence that followed it.

◆　◆　◆　◆

Part of this letter to you, dear Papa, is dedicated to those few witnesses of my life during the war who dared to hold a little girl in safety, even if only for a short time.

The few who helped me were a rare exception in a sea of hostility and indifference. They came, as you'll see, from all walks of life, even the humblest ones. I learned that you don't have to be an aristocrat by blood to belong to a high class of humanity.

◆　◆　◆　◆

As much as I can recall, I'll tell you my story of survival from the moment our dear Janeczka arranged my escape from the Lvov ghetto to the moment your military nurse found me, and took me on this trip to you.

Aunt Jadzia, who on that fateful night took me from the ghetto to her house, was a beautiful woman, medium-sized and well built, with black hair and slightly slanted, almost oriental-looking dark eyes with long black eyelashes. Her skin had a shiny mother-of-pearl appearance. She was a nurse by profession and had two small children. Her husband, who had been a Polish officer before the war, had later escaped via Romania to Spain and then to England, where he became an RAF (Royal Air Force) pilot, recruited by the Polish government in exile in Great Britain. Aunt Jadzia worked for the Polish underground in the Lvov area and had high-level connections on both sides—the underground and the Germans. As we later learned, her feminine charms had given her access to the highest Nazi officials, who were not immune to amorous liaisons with a pretty woman of the so-called lower races, even at the price of giving her secret information. I lived with her for some time, taking care of her children when she was away during the day and after the "witch woman," Pani Wanda, left her home. I cleaned the house, fed the children, and took them for walks to the park. She usually came back late at night and I waited for her to give her report about the day's events. She always told me to avoid meeting with the neighbors and never to talk to them. She lived in a very nice villa, which had been given to her and her husband as a wedding gift by her husband's parents, who had been part of high society in Lvov before the war. One day, Aunt Jadzia brought to her house another Jewish woman named Marlena, who had lost her hiding place with a Polish family; they had taken money and jewelry from her and then denounced her. She had to escape. How she got in touch with my protector I had no idea. She stayed with us no more than three or four days and during that time she did two things memorable to me. One was tragicomic: she decided to change her Semitic appearance and bleached her hair from tarlike black to blonde. When she finished the procedure, she found, to her horror, that she had become a flaming redhead, looking more Jewish than ever before. She was petrified, not knowing what to do. She told me then how lucky I was that I was blond and blue-eyed with a perky Slavic nose. I guess I was lucky that some place, long ago in the past, some of my ancestors had decided to dilute my genetic makeup. Marlena decided to cut off her long, now-red hair almost to the scalp and to wait for her natural color to grow out again. The next day, she told me she was going to some people to buy herself new documents and a new identity. She asked me if I had any fake documents. If not, she said, she had enough money to buy them for me too. She explained that it was important to have some if I got caught. We all—she, Jadzia's children, and I—went by street tram to an Armenian cathedral far away from our house. It was a very old but beautiful building with a tall tower and an inner courtyard surrounded by columns. The city had a large Armenian community who worshiped there and belonged to a very ancient branch of Christianity. An old man in a black priestly vestment took us all to the sacristy, and Marlena conversed with him in the corner. After a while he handed her two envelopes in exchange for gold coins she took out of a small bag hanging inside her blouse. The transaction finished, we went home. She opened one envelope and took out an old-looking, yellowish paper and explained to me that this was my new birth certificate. I was to learn by heart the names not only of my newly acquired parents, but also of my grandparents on both sides of the family, the day

I was born, and, most important, the day I was christened. The paper was supposedly an original document of a child who died prematurely. My new name and names of the fake family were long and strange to my ears. I memorized it all with great difficulty. Fortunately, I never had to pass this test of names—not only would I have failed it, but I also don't think anybody looking at me would have believed I was an Armenian girl.

A short time after the Armenian document episode, Aunt Jadzia gave me some serious news: I would have to leave. A neighbor of hers from a few houses down the street, had told her in a threatening way that she knew Aunt Jadzia was hiding a Jewish girl in her house. Aunt Jadzia had denied it, telling her that I was her relative visiting for a short time. Nevertheless, I would have to go; she would try to arrange some other place for me. The same day she found an oversized warm coat for me, and on a chilly evening took me to her in-laws to stay for a few days. They guessed the truth and agreed to keep me only overnight. The next day she came for me and told me that she was going to try to place me in an orphanage run by Barefoot Carmelite nuns. It was late afternoon when we walked a long way to a different quarter of Lvov, where luxurious houses and villas stood behind ornamental iron fences and gates. To my amazement, we suddenly stopped in front of one of those gates, where a German soldier stood guard. I pulled her hand and wanted to run in panic, thinking that she was going to hand me over to him. She held me tight and said a few words in German to the guard. I didn't understand most of what she said, but I did overhear the name of General Katzman. The soldier let us in. Several steps from the gate, we stood in front of an elaborate entrance door, on the side of which, just above the doorbell, was a golden plate engraved with the same name I had heard a moment before. She rang the bell. After a few seconds a tall man in a black uniform, brown shirt, and black tie opened the door; he stood deep inside. She pulled me quickly in through the half-opened door. I was mute with fear. She turned to me, telling me to sit quietly in the corner chair and wait for her. She followed the SS man through a large room, and they both disappeared from my sight behind the door on the other side of the hall. My instinct told me that I shouldn't be here, but the same instinct prevented me from running. I knew it would not have been successful. My body was stiff with fear, but my eyes were scanning the room. The floor was covered with a multicolored oriental carpet and a desk, a sofa, and a couple of armchairs, all of which were exquisitely beautiful. The only thing that was out of place in this room was me, a little girl with shoes too big for her, an oversized coat, and terrified big eyes. I don't know how long I waited. In circumstances like these, time has no reference to reality. To me, it was an eternity, but I think it was no longer than an hour. When Aunt Jadzia walked into the room again, the man in the SS uniform approached me, touched my cheek with his hand, and said "eine schöne Jude." After that, the two of them embraced briefly, and then Aunt Jadzia and I rapidly walked out. When we were far away from this house she told me, "This man cannot help me to keep you in my house, so we are going to the orphanage I told you about yesterday." My mind was in a maze of confusion, but the warmth of trust and the reassurance of her protection enveloped me again. After all, she hadn't given me away to the man, the same kind of man took my Mama away from me forever.

It was still daylight when we approached a Romanesque-style church to which a big monastery built in red bricks was attached. Before we entered the courtyard of the cloister she gave me the following instructions: first, I was to go to the nuns by myself and explain that I was an orphan and beg them to take me in—she could not go with me because they would not believe the story in her presence. She was sure that they would take me in because they were God-loving and merciful nuns. Her next stern instruction was never to give to anybody, even the nuns, her name or the name of the place where she lived. After that, she embraced me quickly and, wishing me good luck, she disappeared. I didn't see her again until 1947, two years after the war ended. She found you, Papa, and me, and asked for your help in establishing herself in a city in the western part of Poland. Her husband had never come back from England, and she was left with two children to raise alone. I know that you were generous to her, not only in finding her a job, but by helping her financially, sending her money until she and her children were in better circumstances.

I never told you how she left me alone in front of the monastery, because I felt strongly that her desire to protect me as long as she could was truly genuine. I felt then, and still feel, that even the slightest glimmer of compassion should be gratefully acknowledged and honored. Unfortunately, few would deserve it.

✦ ✦ ✦ ✦

The evening was approaching and a cool wind was blowing in my face when I suddenly realized that I had to secure my admission to this orphanage, which I naïvely believed was sure to occur, since I would tell the truth—I *was* an orphan.

I stood in front of a thick, large wooden door, and made a few sharp raps on it with a heavy metal knocker. There was no answer, so I knocked again. After a while a small window opened on one side of the door, and I saw the face and shoulders of a nun dressed in a dark brown habit. After she listened to what I had to say, she asked me to wait until she called a nun superior. She walked away, making noise with her sandals on the cobblestones of the courtyard. As she walked away I saw her bare feet shod in thick leather sandals and connected them with the name of her order, the Barefoot Carmelites. I guess the bareness of their feet was to symbolize their disdain of worldly comforts in complete subjugation to Christian ideals of faith and to all-merciful Jesus, the son of God. I was soon to learn that "mercy" was not their goal.

The next nun who appeared on the other side of the little window started to ask me a long series of questions: "Was I an orphan?"—"Yes." "How old was I?"—"Eleven." "Did I have any family at all?"—"No." She then proceeded to explain to me that they took in only orphans who had lost their parents but still had some kin who would pay the orphanage and support the girl, and then only under the condition that the girl would be prepared to become a nun of this order. (Many years later, I learned that this particular order was one of the richest. It was usually endowed by wealthy aristocratic families whose daughters had disgraced themselves in unworthy sexual liaisons or were ugly enough never to get in one.) When her final question was thrown at me unexpectedly, "Do you want to be a nun?" I said, "No, I never want to be a nun!" There was a short silence. She uttered in a sweet and almost melodic voice, which hangs in my ears even now, "Then go where you came from and God bless you!" The little window closed, and I stood there alone, forsaken by all, and with a sudden understanding that this nun's god, or any god for that matter, was as fake as the Armenian document in my pocket. He would never invoke any divine care for me. The nun's words, "God bless you," really meant that God had no blessings to give.

◆　◆　◆　◆

Night was falling, and it was getting colder; the wind was no more, and the sky burst with tiny diamond speckles. I remember distinctly that on that night I did not cry. I don't even think I allowed myself a feeling of loneliness or self-pity. In retrospect I think some inner spark of energy took over to summon all my childish smartness or wild animal's instinct, or something akin to this that stray dogs or feral cats display. I knew I would have to use those tricks of nature for an indefinite time, to survive.

I was walking in the direction of the center of the city, where there were more people on the street. The street lamps were sparse, and in between them was pitch-dark night. I was so tired that I decided to find a place to sleep. I walked into an apartment building and climbed the stairs to the top until they ended in a dark garret, a dark room just below the sloping roof. Lying down on hard wooden planks, I fell asleep. From then on for a long time, those garrets and attics became not only bedrooms, but also escapes and hiding places when I was chased by people shouting, "Catch this Jewess!

This name was my curse, a name that only three or four years ago I hadn't known the meaning of but that now meant danger and a signal to run. During the days, I spent time hunting for scraps of food, mostly in trash bins. What I found were potato peels or spoiled vegetables and bones with scarce leftover remnants of meat on them. One day I discovered a place where good food was falling down, almost literally, straight from the sky. On the outskirts of the city, which by now I had started to know well, I found three-story-tall army barracks stretching for several blocks, occupied by Hungarian soldiers, allies of the Germans at that time. Many of them were sitting in the windows and throwing food to children gathered on the sidewalk beneath. What a discovery that was! We filled our pockets with fresh pieces of bread, candies, and sometimes even apples. The soldiers were laughing and shouted some words in a language none of us understood. When the handout was over, the mothers of all the other children would walk them away from this place, and I would run as fast as I could so as not to give away the fact that I had no mother waiting for me.

Days and weeks and months were passing as I endlessly wandered the streets, always with the same aim—to find some food and shelter for the night.

My body was dirty, my hair and clothes infested with lice, which I was unable to get rid of, only easing their parasitic invasion upon me with constant scratching, leaving bloody marks on my skin.

The early winter was upon us. It was severe that year, making it even harder to survive. My shoes got big holes in the soles, and I patched them daily with pieces of paper or rugs found on the streets or in the trash. My stockings were full of holes. The only piece of clothing that was still relatively intact was the oversized coat given to me by Aunt Jadzia long ago.

Calendar or clock had no meaning for me. My time was measured by dawn, dusk, and night, by sunshine, rain, snow, or wind. Calendar names of days or months or years had no relevance for me either. I set myself to survive between one sunrise and sunset at a time and started my voyage of despair anew upon the next sunrise. Sometimes, I remember, I would pass by, in the evening, close to the window of some basement apartments—they were called in Polish *suteryna,* from the French, *sous terrain,* meaning "underground." These basements were occupied by the poorest members of society, but what I saw, stopping in front of those windows, was the ultimate luxury of a family, sitting by the table in warmth and light, having supper together. Sometimes a smell of cooked stew or freshly baked bread would reach my nostrils. This unattainable, simple happiness usually evoked in me such a strong yearning that I would run away from this vision, feeling that I might collapse there and maybe even die. I promised myself that when I grew up and the war ended—for some reason I believed that both of these things would happen: I would grow up, and the war would end—I would have such a basement apartment from which would emanate the smells of fresh baked bread and cooked stew.

Yes, Papa, you eventually provided for me much more, and a lot of material luxury to compensate my misery, but this lit basement window and the smell of food remains with me as a bittersweet memory forever.

There were plenty of people around me in those terrible times. They were on the streets, in the houses, in the trams, in the churches. I knew, however, how to be as invisible as I could. I knew instinctively and from experience to hide from them; most of them were not the right people, and being close to them was dangerous.

I also knew that although never in my short life had I done any harm to anybody, for some mysterious reason they hated me.

✦ ✦ ✦ ✦

One day, a Sunday, I was shuffling my feet on the pavement, in shoes too big for me that I had been lucky to find the day before, discarded by someone in the park. I was glad because the shoes didn't have holes in the soles and my feet were warm and dry. I knew it was Sunday because minutes before, the bells of a nearby church had been ringing, announcing midday. A lot of people were moving toward the church for Sunday mass. I accidentally brushed my body against a tall, skinny man going in the opposite direction with a young woman holding his arm. He looked at me angrily, then grabbed my shoulder to halt me. I didn't expect it, but I knew this was a signal for me to run. I tore myself free from him and ran as fast as I could, but the man ran after me and I heard him shouting, "Catch this little Jew!" I blended in with the crowd, but when I quickly looked back, I saw the man standing by a German gendarme, pointing in my direction. I ran even faster and reached the church's gate just in time to mix with a tight crowd already there. I knew this church intimately; it was a magnificent, baroque-style shrine with a big dome encrusted with shiny tiles. It was named after Saint Bernard, Katedra Bernardynska.

I forgot to tell you, Papa, that besides the garrets and attics of big apartment houses, churches were also my sleeping retreats. They were open twenty-four hours and usually were built so that in addition to the nave—the central part of the church—they had side alcoves or small chapels dedicated to different patron saints. These niches were recessed deep enough to accommodate a few pews for prayers. Sometimes they were large enough to have additional altars for conducting masses dedicated to one particular saint. I slept in many churches around the city. The bigger ones were safer and easier to hide in. I always slept under the pew, making sure that my legs and arms didn't stick out. Sometimes a couple of books with psalms taken out of the wooden pocket in the pew served me as a pillow. Small churches were warmer because the doors were smaller, allowing less air movement. More important, the floors were wooden and not so cold as the marble or stone floors in big cathedrals and rich parishes. The permanent smell of incense hanging in the air was a calming, sedating aura to my mind and body, easing me into slumber. When I told you I knew the churches intimately, I was not making it up.

This time, on this particular Sunday, I pushed myself to the third row of the pews and with my head bowed down, I pretended to pray while the priest, in a special, gold-decorated vestment, conducted the mass, with four altar boys as the helpers in the ritual. Suddenly, there was a commotion in the back of the church and two German gendarmes appeared, one walking toward the altar through the main aisle, the other surveying the pews from the side passages. The priest did not interrupt his prayers, all in Latin, and frequently turned from the altar toward the worshipers, making a sign of the cross with his hand and gestures blessing the audience, who repeated from time to time in unison, the one word I knew: Amen. The word was always stretched a bit on the last syllable, so it sounded like an end of a song.

The two gendarmes were still in the church. When it came time for communion, when those who confessed to their sins in the confessional booth were allowed to partake in this ritual. Many stood up from the pews and lined up to get in the front of the altar, and, while kneeling, to swallow a wafer offered by the priest, followed with a sip of wine. I stood up with the others, and when my turn came I partook in this ritual, mimicking exactly the movements and gestures of crossing myself as all the other faithful Catholics did. I participated in the symbolic ritual of eating the god's flesh and drinking his blood without any regrets for being sinful. Even if I had preceded it by confession, I didn't have any sins to confess, and more truthfully, I was ignorant of the meaning of this word. This was not the last time I participated in this ceremonial rite; I will tell you about it later.

There's an old folk saying, "God protects those who protect themselves." In a twisted kind of way, it applied to me on that winter Sunday.

There was one small occurrence in the scheme of things that I want to describe to you, not because it was a life-altering experience, but because it might give you a glimpse into your little girl's state of mind.

One day, I was sitting on the edge of a gutter, resting my feet after a long walk to nowhere, a walk that was my only occupation in those days. It was an aimless rest of necessity. A big cat approached me with a mouse hanging from his mouth. He was sitting in front of me delighting in the finishing of his catch. I could have easily chased him away from his feast and made him share with me this warm piece of food. The eyes of the mouse were wide open, the body twitching although the bloody insides were already on the ground. It was, however, beyond my capability, despite my ever-present hunger, to satisfy it with this bloody mess. The rotten, reeking food I gathered with great difficulty was as far as I could go in my human degradation. I wonder how you would explain that?

◆　◆　◆　◆

There were three other things I did not do during that time. I did not beg, I did not cry, and I did not steal. I don't think this was a result of some earlier inculcated morality or nobility. In my world, I needed to be a shadow, an invisible disembodied soul. All three of those activities were dangerous and would bring forth more hate, and I would have to defend myself against it. Was it intelligence, instinct, or both—who knows? I didn't cry because my tears had dried out. The last time I had cried was on the night when the peasant took me, hidden in a horse-drawn buggy, back to Mama, shortly after I witnessed the macabre slaughter in Radjekov.

◆　◆　◆　◆

The train was moving fast toward my destination—my father—and with fewer stops. We were in Russia now. The fields were empty and covered with snow, and occasionally we could see small hamlets of cottages with straw-covered roofs. Here and there a thin, gray smoke would weave itself from the chimneys, blending into the gray sky—a sign of life. The train was getting less crowded since more and more people disembarked on the way. At some point there was even an empty bench in our compartment on which I could stretch out and sleep all night. This space was given to me, as the only child there, by four women sitting on the opposite bench, and your nurse, sitting at my feet. This was a welcomed kindness from strangers—a rarity in my recent past and a sign of hope that I could be a child again, with the privileges of childhood. There was so much to tell you and the images were crowding my head to the clickety-click music of the train's wheels.

◆　◆　◆　◆

Let's then go back to Lvov, the place of my pilgrimage of despair and sorrow. On one sleety evening, I was sitting stooped on a threshold of a building in wet clothes, shivering from cold. My life would have probably ended there, my body tired, my mind too worn out even to care. I woke up from a kind of stupor when a woman bent over me and asked me my name. I told her my real name. Seeing my gruesome, shivering state, she helped me to stand up and told me that she lived a few houses from there, and that she would take me to her home. Her voice was reassuring, or so I wished to believe. The only thing I knew for sure at this point was that I needed to be inside, away from the cold. After a few steps we entered a tall building and then a narrow corridor.

Passing by a fancy marble staircase, we went through a small courtyard and entered a very small hall with a winding iron staircase of the type you usually see in narrow towers of lighthouses. When we reached the top floor, there was a narrow balcony circling the space of the courtyard visible five stories below us.

This woman's apartment was close to the iron staircase. She opened it with a key and we entered a fairly large room. In the middle of the room was a big dinner table with four chairs, to the left was a big kitchen stove. She helped me take off my soaking, cold, wet clothes and shoes, wrapped me in a big towel, and, while putting a pot of water on the stove in preparation for my bath, took out bread, sausage, and bottles of beer from her bag. She put all those riches on the table in front of me, cut pieces of bread and sausage for me to eat, then opened a bottle of beer and told me to take two sips from the bottle, saying, "It will do you good." All this was done quickly. I looked on almost as a detached being, watching a movie on the screen. The taste of the beer was bitter and repulsive, but as it reached my empty stomach I felt a warmth radiating through my body.

After I ate, she poured the warm water from the pot into a small portable metal tub and before letting me sit in it she inspected my hair and clothes for lice. Obviously she expected me to be lice-infested, knowing the condition she found me in. As you know very well, Papa, the louse is the best-thriving and most prosperous human parasite during wartime. She put all my clothes in a bag, to be disposed of in the trash, and poured kerosene on my hair, rubbing it into the skin of my skull. She then covered my hair with a tight cap. This hair procedure, she said, would be repeated three times to delouse me completely.

All this done, she showed me the room next to the stove where I would sleep. The room was windowless, dark, without an electric lamp in it. There was a cot with one pillow and a blanket and one chair in it. While I was in bed, she told me her name was Kazia, short for Kazimiera, and that in the morning she would tell me all the things I would need to know while staying with her. I don't think I heard the last words she said. I was already fast asleep.

The happenings of that evening some would call a divine providence. I say that acts of human nobility come sometimes from unexpected places.

I told you about Kazia after the war, but not in such detail as now. I remember insisting that you, Papa, try to find her, but she had perished and could be brought to life only through my memories of her.

◆   ◆   ◆   ◆

Kazia was short and chubby. Her legs were bowed by childhood rickets, so that when she stood with her feet close together, both of her shins formed an elongated letter *O*. Her face looked like a triangle, the base of which was her protruding forehead. Her eyes were very small and set unusually far apart. Her nose had no base, only the tip of it protruded upwardly with big nostrils prominently displayed—it looked altogether like a horse's saddle. She had narrow lips that never completely covered her large upper front teeth, which were big and yellow with serrated edges. Her hair was light brown, and she wore short bangs. By all the standards of feminine beauty, she was very ugly. She presented a perfect picture of Hutchinson's triad, a syndrome befalling people with congenital syphilis characterized in medical books by notched incisors, saddle nose, and diffuse inflammation of the cornea (keratitis). This became obvious to me later, while a student in medical school. The disease is passed in the uterus from a syphilitic mother to her baby.

Just from her external appearance one could deduce her unhappy childhood, forged upon her by the callousness of fate. There arose a peculiar friendship between this thirty-two-year-old woman and an eleven-year-old girl, who in prewar Poland probably would never have met.

Kazia worked in a beer tavern, situated on the first floor of a City Hall now called *radhaus* (in Polish, *ratusz*), where she served beer to German soldiers and officers who were the only customers there. She earned very little money as a barmaid, so she supplemented her income and softened her life in two ways: she stole beer and food from the Germans who ran the tavern, and she sold her body, its ugliness no deterrent to drunken German soldiers.

Almost every day she would bring home in two big bags made of thick fabric a dozen or more bottles of beer, which she then distributed to her own clientele for good money. Once or twice, sometimes three times in the week, she would bring a German soldier, usually of no or low rank, into her house for carnal pleasures in exchange for deutsche marks.

She trusted me, so I became her helper, delivering beer to her customers in different parts of the city; in order not to raise any suspicion, she bought me nice, warm clothes and shoes, so I looked like a legitimate "Aryan" kid.

When she brought her drunken lovers to the house, usually at night, she would lock me up in my windowless niche until they vanished outside into the night. I must admit, I was curious about their activity, especially when some unusual voices and noises filtered through the walls and doors to my ears. However, my curiosity was always dampened by a much stronger feeling— the fear of Germans. So I never opened my door or gave any sign of life, and usually fell asleep, awakened by Kazia in the morning with good news—food. In the meantime, in Kazia's care I was clean, deloused, and warm. The frostbite on my knees and feet healed, my cheeks became fuller and rosy again, and I gained weight. I also noticed that I grew a little, judging by the height of the doorknobs relative to the height of my body.

On some evenings, when Kazia didn't have her men guests, we would sit at the table and she would tell me some stories from her miserable childhood and teens. Her mother had been an alcoholic and a prostitute who had syphilis and died in an insane asylum; after she'd had Kazia, she gave birth to two stillborn babies. Kazia never knew who her father was. There were moments when I listened to all this stuff and I felt that her life was infinitely more sad than mine. At least I had some sun-drenched memories to fall back on in my worst times and a faint flicker of hope that something better might lie ahead. She had neither. I was not afraid to tell her about my life before the war, about Mama and you and my sister—I knew she would not betray me. It was always puzzling to me that when she heard about my life, she would interrupt my stories, exclaiming "You poor little girl!" as if to say, "You had and then lost so much goodness. I had nothing so precious to lose; thus I feel more sorrow for you than for myself."

◆　◆　◆　◆

You remember, Papa, my description of the house that I first entered with Kazia, after she found me half-frozen and numb. There was the wide, marble staircase with fancy handrails. The staircase led to the apartments in the front of the house with windows facing the street. These were very elegant apartments now occupied only by Ukrainian families after the prewar owners, some Polish, some Jewish, were expelled: the former forcefully evicted, the latter marched to the ghetto and then killed in extermination camps.

Kazia told me to be wary of the people who lived there; they were mean and tolerated her presence in the back of the house only because they knew she was bringing German soldiers there. I was always to be very careful to sneak out of the house unnoticed, especially when carrying the stolen German beer to sell.

◆　◆　◆　◆

If I remember correctly, the winter was coming to an end, but it wasn't spring yet. By that time, I had been living with Kazia for several weeks. Compared to my homeless life on the streets before she took me in, it was an almost idyllic and peaceful time. The daily routine imposed on me by her lifestyle pushed the fear of being caught and killed to the back of my mind.

One day, I was coming back after delivering a few bottles of beer to Kazia's customers. I had the empty bag in my hand and was climbing the narrow spiral stairs at a relaxed pace when I was suddenly accosted by a fat young man descending in the opposite direction. I tried to pass him and continue on my way up, but he pushed me with his fist, and I fell on one of the steps. He started to kick my body, stomach, chest, and legs and punched my head, face, and neck with his fist. The kicking and punching wasn't fast, but was deliberate and determined to do me harm. While he was beating me, he talked to me in a squeaky voice, saying that he knew I was a Jew and had been hiding someplace in this building. He demanded that I tell him where, and when I didn't answer, his fat face came closer to mine and he spit on me. In a reflex to avoid blows to my face and head, I curled up the way porcupines do, hiding my face and head close to my stomach. I never uttered a word and imagined only two possible outcomes of my sudden misfortune—I would be killed, or he would go away. His sadistic desire satisfied—I say sadistic because I'm sure he didn't expect to find any riches on me—he suddenly stopped beating me and said in Ukrainian that he was leaving now, but if he found me on these stairs again tomorrow, he would kill me. What an idiot! I thought, why would I be here tomorrow? I knew how to run and hide from people like him! But I couldn't move, the pain in my whole body was keeping me in an iron vice. So I stayed there, unable to move, expecting only the worst to come, when I heard the noise of somebody coming up. I was sure it was him again but still couldn't move! In a few moments, I saw Kazia approaching me. In one, all-knowing glance, she understood what had happened. She picked me up and, begging me not to cry, she took me to her apartment. While cleaning me up and wiping off some blood from my legs, she told me that at night she would take me to a woman she knew, who knew a man who would help me.

And so she did. The two women, Kazia and her friend, waited with me in the friend's house until the next morning, when a man dressed in gray pants tucked into high boots, wearing a flat cap on his head, showed up. They all agreed that he would take me immediately to a hiding place. Kazia squeezed my hand and said, "Don't give up, and stay in good health." I saw a few silent tears sliding down Kazia's cheeks—she was losing a semblance of the family she had never had. After this short good-bye, the man took me with him.

Later, I learned that Kazia did survive the war. When on the way back from Russia we stopped in Lvov, both of us went to the house where I had lived with her, and we were told by the neighbors that she had moved to another city.

◆　◆　◆　◆

Because of my bruises and aching muscles, I couldn't walk too fast or for long periods of time, so we sat several times on street benches and rested. The man asked what my first name was, and I told him Helenka. Then he told me that he was taking me to an orphanage run by nuns. I told him that he was wasting his time, because I didn't have any money or family to pay the nuns—and, most of all, I didn't want to be a nun when I grew up. The nuns wouldn't accept me. I knew because I had tried it once and they had closed the door in my face. When I finished he smiled and said that he knew of such nuns, but he knew much better ones. This time, I smiled, and all-knowingly said, "We will see who is right!" Fortunately, I was wrong.

◆　◆　◆　◆

We finally reached the outskirts of the city, where houses were smaller, separated by large gardens and trees. The trees were naked at this time of the year, and I could see the sky through an intricate, fine, lacy design of their leafless branches.

Soon we entered one of those gardens, framed by a picket fence. At the end of the path stood a fairly large, two-story house, painted light gray. The man knocked on the door and asked the nun who opened it to lead him to the mother superior. When we entered her office, she stood up from behind the desk and greeted the man by his first name; obviously she knew him well. A few words were exchanged between them, and then he said, "I want to leave this little girl with you. She has no place to stay." Mother Superior just nodded her head slightly in a gesture of acceptance. He let my hand go, bowed deeply, and left. This short encounter of the man with the nun looked to me almost like a rehearsed theatrical scene where I had a mute and silent role. When the man left, Mother Superior asked my name and told me to sit down on the chair and wait for her—she would be back shortly.

She came back with a nun, Sister Stanislava, who took me to a large room with several long narrow tables behind which were seated rows of girls. She introduced me to this crowd of girls by my name and announced that I would be staying here permanently. She then chose one much older girl, Marianna, to be my mentor and teach me everything I needed to know about the life in the orphanage.

◆ ◆ ◆ ◆

The orphanage was run by nuns of the Holy Mother of Mercy order. The only areas of skin visible on the nuns were their faces and hands. The rest of their bodies were hidden under black, floor-length habits, a type of dress probably worn by medieval women. I thought the habit was very beautiful but difficult to describe in its essential simplicity; It was a loose black dress, with wide sleeves and deep pockets on each side. Each nun's face and neck was framed by a stiff, heavily starched white fabric, which also formed a square visor extending about two inches from the top of the forehead, shading her face like the eave of a roof. A black veil was attached to the head covering and floated down to below the waist in a rich cascade of fabric lighter than that of the habit, so when the nuns walked at a quicker pace, it moved in a graceful wave. The nuns wore silver rings on their fingers as a symbol of being wed to their faith. They also wore big, simple wooden crosses about three inches long, suspended on thick silver chains around their necks.

Four nuns were directly involved with the running of the orphanage and managing the girls. Mother Superior was the spiritual leader and also a judge when controversies or squabbles between girls needed to be resolved. She was an older woman with a wrinkled face and glasses. Next in importance was Sister Stanislava. She was like an administrator organizing our work. She provided our supplies; she was also a liaison between the remaining nuns and Mother Superior. She was tall, robust, and energetic, moving in big steps in a manly fashion. She was liked by all of the girls for her no-nonsense and just decisions. Just the opposite of her was Sister Katarzyna, petite with a pretty face, big blue eyes, and a girlish voice. She was our catechism teacher, instructing us in Catholic doctrine. The fourth nun was Sister Veronika, whom my mentor Mariana warned me to avoid if possible because she was a "mean old woman."

There were also other nuns who worked in the kitchen or in the laundry, who cleaned the house and the chapel, or who worked in the big garden in the back of the monastery, growing their own vegetables. On that first day, I also learned that, including me, there were thirty-six girls of different ages in the orphanage, of whom I was the youngest. I was shown two rooms, one with twenty-four metal beds, where I would be sleeping, and another where the twelve older girls had their beds. We went with Sister Stanislava to a storage room where they chose a uniform and underwear for me—much too big, but the smallest available. While I was changing the nun noticed the bruises and scratches on my body and she said that I would have two days of rest before they show me what kind of work I would be doing.

This was my first day in the orphanage, which for all I knew would be my home forever.

Over the several months of my life I spent in the orphanage I had to absorb quickly new experiences and new routines.

I went to sleep, like everybody else, about ten o'clock at night in the huge twenty-four-bed dormitory after a prayer said in unison. My first night there, my body was invaded by bedbugs—round, brownish-red parasites that I discovered in the morning crawling all over me, swollen with my blood, which explained the terrible itching I had felt all night. The girls told me that I had to put the four legs of the bed in four bowls filled with water with some vinegar in it, so the bedbugs trying to crawl up the legs of my bed would drown in those bowls. And indeed, I then noticed that all the other beds had such arrangements. My roommates also told me that I should spread one sheet over my body like a canopy, attaching the sheet to the four metal posters of the bed. They said that the bugs were very smart and, failing to reach the bed through the water and vinegar defense, would crawl up the walls of the room to the ceiling, and from there parachute onto our warm bodies.

In the morning, the wake-up time announced by a nun with a hand-held metal bell was five o'clock. We washed our faces and hands in small washbowls using so-called laundry soap, which was yellow, bad-smelling, hard as a brick, slightly oily, and never produced any foam. We washed our teeth with a wet index finger. I must tell you that this was already progress in my hygiene because I had not brushed my teeth since my escape from the ghetto hospital; I never had a toothbrush. After the skimpy washing, bathing of the whole body was done once a week on Saturdays, when we worked only until noon.

We began the day with a morning prayer in the chapel consisting of the litany to the saints. Breakfast was served in the same room where, after cleaning the tables, we worked. The morning meal consisted of kasha with a few drops of oil floating on the top, a piece of dark bread, and water. We could ask for seconds. On Sundays, instead of water, we had a cup of hot milk. The nuns had two cows, which they milked daily. They sold the milk on the black market.

After breakfast, all of us worked. The older girls sewed linens, pillow covers, aprons, and other household articles, which the nuns sold for money or exchanged for food, mostly flour or meat. The younger girls, me among them, made buttons for the bed linens produced there. I learned very quickly how to make those buttons and in a short time could produce two or three dozen of them, depending on the size, in a workday. The buttons were made with thick white thread woven in an intricate way around a flat metal ring. I made so many of them, that I'm sure that even now I could reproduce them without any difficulty. In fact, just this evening, sixty years later, I made a copy of such a button.

◆　◆　◆　◆

Just after a midday rest of an hour, we had dinner, which routinely was a vegetable or potato soup and bread.

The work then resumed until about eight o'clock in the evening, when we stopped for supper, usually a sandwich with lard and slices of onions. On Sundays, two spoonfuls of scrambled eggs would be added to our menu.

As you see, the monastery and the orphanage was self-sufficient, a well-organized enterprise with a lot of smart initiatives on the part of the nuns that allowed them to survive and feed the orphans in their charge. They had only a little help from the church hierarchy.

The only time we were outside in fresh air was when we took turns in helping with the vegetable garden or cleaning the barn or the chicken coop.

On Saturday afternoons and Sunday mornings, a priest would come to hear our confessions. All the girls were obliged to confess, because all of us would have to partake at midday of Sunday mass and Holy Communion.

As you remember, my first experience with this ritual was at the Saint Bernard cathedral, when I successfully escaped the German gendarmes. I would now repeat it every Sunday.

The communion was easy. I just had to swallow this symbolic body and blood of the god worshiped by the nuns, to whom I felt no obligation since I couldn't find any role this god played in my life. All the teachings about this god and the tenets of the Catholic religion were delivered to us by the pretty Sister Katarzyna. She repeated over and over again that we were to accept any suffering, pain, or sorrow as a divine and mysterious plan that this god had for us all. Even a small, uneducated girl like me could not excuse the cruelty I had witnessed in the ghetto—the loss of Mama and Janka, my exile into the cold loneliness and hunger—or make a connection between such experiences and this god's mysterious and divine plan. I complied with all the rules and rites, but I believed none of it.

Communion was an easy task, but I had a problem with confession: I couldn't come up with any sins I had committed. I asked my mentor, Marianna, what I should tell the priest hidden in the wooden booth of the confessional. She gave me some good advice and examples of "sins" that I confessed to repeatedly, trivialities that never occupied my mind—never mind that the lying itself was a sin. Examples of sins I confessed:

• I didn't finish a prayer;

• During a mass, I was thinking of a princess-like dress I would like to wear;

• I was jealous of some girl being prettier than me.

Don't you think, Papa, that from the perspective of time, all this is, in a twisted sort of way, ludicrous and funny?

All in all, however, I was grateful to the nuns for life in the orphanage. I was warm, not hungry, had a roof over my head, was treated the same as all the other girls, and, most important of all, I didn't have to run and hide. It is also remarkable that I never witnessed or was aware of any corporal punishment being delivered to any of the girls for misbehavior. The name of the order, Holy Mother of Mercy, was justified in my mind. I learned that, as well as providing safety to thirty-six orphans, Mother Superior had hidden three other Jewish girls in the monastery. Another proof of her commitment to Mercy (with a capital M) was one "girl" who was thirty-two years old by the time I arrived there. Blind from birth, she had been dropped off at the doorstep of the monastery as a little girl. As she grew up, it was obvious she was also mentally retarded. She lived with the nuns, who took care of her, and we all were taught how to help her with her daily activities.

But one episode revealed to me that, despite their professed faith and vocation, not all nuns were created equal.

One evening, Sister Veronika, who was the supervisor of our work and the one described to me on the first day as a mean old woman to be wary of, announced to all of us at the end of the workday that some clothes had been stolen from a storage room. She demanded a confession from whomever did it before we went to our beds. No one moved. We were silent and didn't look at one another. She became angry and shouted that she had a way to find the truth and the thief. She made us all sit at the tables, then set glasses full of water and straws of equal length in front of us. She ordered us to put one end of the straw in the glass and the other end in our mouths; when this was done she turned out the light, and in complete darkness, her voice sounding ominous, she said that whichever of us did the stealing would be revealed. The devil would make the straw of the guilty one grow rapidly in length. This macabre and scary scene lasted several minutes, after which she turned on the lights again and went from girl to girl, collecting the straws and checking their length. I must admit, I didn't believe in God, but about the devil's nonexistence I wasn't so sure. I had one moment of hesitation, wondering if I shouldn't bite off a piece of the straw in case "he," the devil, had made it grow in my glass. I didn't, but one skinny, scared girl did. She was punished by Sister Veronika by two days of fasting and solitude in a dark cell, from which a faint sobbing was heard through the walls. A few days later, after this nun's exercise in sadistic psychology and justice, it was discovered that a nun working in the kitchen had taken the clothes. Sister Veronika never apologized or consoled the skinny girl; she just gave her a warning not to listen to the devil's advice. This "straw" episode showed me that saintly habits can cover very ugly souls.

◆ ◆ ◆ ◆

As I told you before, Mother Superior and Sister Stanislava were the only ones who knew why I was in this orphanage. Observing my behavior and compliance with all the rules of life there, including the religious ones, they suggested on several occasions that I could be baptized there. This would be the ultimate salvation, not only of my body but also of my soul. Being baptized, they explained to me, would mean that when I died, I would be admitted to heaven and permanently joined with their god. For reasons I explained to you before, I didn't like their god and didn't want to spend eternity in his company. It must be counted in their favor that they never forced me into this ritual, and in my favor that I never consented to it. I must admit I still hold a deep respect for the little girl who was "I" at that time.

◆ ◆ ◆ ◆

The monastery was located on the northwestern outskirts of the city. For several days, the noises of cannons and gunfire were heard from the east. Skies painted with fire could be seen from the same direction. There was a palpable anxiety bordering on panic among the nuns that spread by contagion to the thirty-six orphans. Then the noises of war ceased. Word came to us that the Germans had retreated rapidly to the west and the Russian army had reoccupied the city.

One day Mother Superior collected the Jewish girls in her office and told us about the ruins of the synagogue, where we could put our names announcing our survival. You know the rest of the story, except that after being temporarily adopted by the dentist lady, I returned to Mother Superior to tell her about my new home. She and Sister Stanislava blessed me with the sign of the cross, and this was the only time they allowed me to embrace them in silent gratitude for their goodness, which I will always remember.

◆　◆　◆　◆

When I lived with you in Russia, we both wrote a long letter to Mother Superior expressing our gratitude for the safety she and her nuns provided for me. To our joyful surprise, she answered with a long letter, of which I remember one sentence very well. She wrote how happy she was that I had found my "earthly father" and she hoped that one day I would also find the "heavenly one." I knew that her wishes for me were heartfelt, but I also knew that the "earthly" one was all that I wanted and needed.

◆　◆　◆　◆

The war ended in May 1945. When we were returning to Poland in 1946, you made a special effort to pass through the city of Lvov on our journey. The two of us went to see the nuns but found the monastery empty. The nuns of the order of Holy Mother of Mercy had been evacuated to the western part of Poland with all the other Polish nationals who chose not to stay in what was now the Ukrainian Soviet Republic.

I also know that for many years you sent anonymous donations to the orphanage in its new location, and I will always be thankful to you for it.

◆ ◆ ◆ ◆

The long journey to the faraway city in Russia came to an end on a cold winter evening, when the conductor of the train loudly and repeatedly announced, while passing through the corridors of the wagons, *Gorod Penza!* City of Penza! There was no chance that anyone who needed to disembark would miss the stop, thanks to his cries. My heart was pounding in anticipation for many hours before this stop, and now it was ready to jump from my skinny rib cage. What if this were the wrong city? What if you forgot to come? What if this was all a delusion and I was left standing on the platform again, alone and at the mercy of strangers?

These thoughts were as rapid as lightning in my head and as loud as a clap of thunder. The emissary nurse took my hand, and we walked out onto a crowded platform. People in thick coats and furry caps were shoving and pushing, talking loudly, creating whispery white little clouds around their mouths as the warm air coming from their lungs condensed in the freezing air. And there you were, Papa, clothed in the same manner, your sunken cheeks covered with short bristles of silver, unshaven hair.

You ran toward me and picked me up from the platform as one picks up a baby. I was a big girl by then, but as you held me tightly in your arms, my feet hung down below your knees. I felt, despite the frozen air around us, the warmth of the blanket you used to put around me before I fell asleep so many years ago. I knew at that moment that I would be allowed to be a child again. Papa, years later, after I moved to America, I wish I could have greeted you the same way. But you felt you were too old to exchange your life for a new one, and you chose to stay behind

in Poland. You died of heart failure at the age of seventy-six, in 1974, thirty years after the war's end.

I thank you, dear Papa, for your greeting of love at the railway station, and for the many years of privileged indulgence you provided for me in your endless desire to erase and compensate me for my past misery.

Always your little girl,
Helunia

Commentary

＊　＊　＊　＊

As I finished the last of the three letters recalling the first twelve years of my life and the events that shaped them, many thoughts crowded into my mind.

They were not new. I had rehashed them endlessly throughout my adult life, aided by an acquired knowledge of history, psychology, philosophy, and a continuation of life experiences.

It would be almost impossible for me to summarize them, to describe them, to organize them without emotional involvement; thus I decided to reduce those thoughts to only a few numerical facts. What follows are my private and personal statistics:

• At the start of World War II, the population of Poland was close to 32 million people.

• It was a country of my ancestors for at least six hundred years.

• At the time of the German invasion, thirty-three members of my immediate and extended family were living in Poland.

• Out of those thirty-three, only one survived, namely, me.

• Not counting my mother, my sister Janka, and my mother's far-removed niece, five people (five!) actively participated in saving my life: Aunt Jadwiga, the Polish nurse; Kazia—formally, Kazimiera—the Polish prostitute; Mother Superior of the Holy

Mother of Mercy order, a Polish nun; Doctor Litvak, the Jewish director of the Lvov ghetto hospital; and a nameless member of the Gestapo, a German.

- The time involved in those active acts of mercy ranged from a few seconds to several weeks.
- Of my saviors listed above, all three members of Polish society survived the war.
- The fate of the Gestapo man is unknown to me, but the possibility exists that he survived too.
- The Jewish doctor perished in the extermination camp of Belzec.

This is the briefest and most concise way I am able to judge those infamous times. It is brief indeed . . . but profoundly telling.

◆　◆　◆　◆

With due humility and some pride, I not only accepted the survival of my body, but also celebrated the survival of my spirit as often as I could.

Traveling across California in June 1987, I wrote this poem:

Flowers, colors and flowers,
Blossoms on a velvet of grass
   Covering the planet.
The wind's aroma,
Excitement of the unknown . . .
Red, yellow and sunset,
The vapors of flowers in the sky—
   A rainbow over the planet!
Hands reaching for flowers,
Hands reaching for rainbow . . .
   Don't touch!
   Let it be!
Fragile fragrance of colors,
Trembling to last forever.

In my eyes: red, yellow,
    Sunset and . . . night.
In the morning—anew
    Excitement,
    Aroma,
    Unknown . . .
And velvet of grass that is pregnant
With rainbows of flowers again.
Galactic perpetuum mobile!
    Don't touch!
    Let it be!
Viva the planet! Surviving in chaos!
Trembling to last forever.
For reasons obscure to my mind,
I welcome this tremor of life.

My mother and sister, Lvov, c. 1925

My mother and sister, Warez, first house,
c. 1928

My mother, 1935

My sister, mother, and I, Lvov, 1938

My father, sister and I, Lvov, c. 1938

My sister, my friend, and I, with Bambi, my fox
terrier, Warez, July 1938

My sister, Lvov, 1938

Janka and I, Warez, October 1938

New house built in 1936, Warez, October 1938

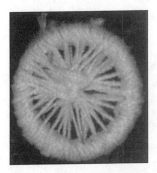

Button made by author in manner taught her by the nuns of the Holy Mother of Mercy order

Olga in her twenties or early thirties, Moscow, c. 1930

Olga and I, Penza, Russia, 1944

The ruins of our home in 1944, Warez. Photo made in 1956

Letter to My Stepmother

• • • •

Dear Olik,

The first time I saw you was the night Papa took me from the train station in a truck from his hospital, with a uniformed Russian driver, to the two-story, L-shaped house in which you lived with him. After climbing the tall staircase and going through a long hall, we entered a room crowded with furniture, which had very little free space.

"This is Olga Aleksandrovna," Papa said to me.

I had always had a penchant to invent terms of endearment for those people close to my heart, as if to say they were mine or, even more truly, that we belonged to each other. Thus, "Olik" was the name I invented for you. This happened some time—actually, a long time—after our first meeting.

That wintry evening, when I found my father at the railroad station of the city of Penza, deep in the interior territory of Russia, was the beginning of a new stage in my life. In this stage, dear Olga, as in a theatrical drama, you and I played an important role in mutually discovering the way to trust, in finding a narrow, treacherous path to a deep connection. The delicacy of our feelings was tested as we climbed the rocky road of our life together, but in the end we were gratified by twenty-four years of mutual love and deep friendship.

Allow me to recall all the facts as I received them in that winter of 1944.

Your name was Olga Aleksandrovna Archipova. The second name was given to adult women and men, by old Russian custom, from the name of their fathers. As an adult woman, I would be called Yelena (from Helena) Lvovna (from my father's name Lev, translated from the Polish Leon, which, by the way, derived from the Latin word *leo*, meaning "lion").

You were born in 1896 to the rather higher class of Russian society that existed before the 1917 revolution. Your mother belonged to the landed gentry, and your father was a physician in the tsar's army with the high rank of colonel. He died a few years after the Russo-Japanese war of 1905, in which he participated.

I am sure it would be a pleasure for you to know that I have in my house in California a few beautiful souvenirs your father brought from the Far East, which by now are antiques more than one hundred years old. Yes, your Lenochka displays them, together with your few old Russian icons, as palpable reminders of you. Literally palpable, because when I touch them, my hands are meeting the fingerprints of your touch.

Your mother died in the early 1920s, but before that event you moved to Moscow, the ancient capital of Russia, where you started your higher education in 1915 at the age of nineteen. You attended Moscow University for Women, studying history and philosophy. In prerevolutionary Russia, this was most certainly a desired education for a young girl, as a preparation for life in higher society.

I have in front of me an official booklet issued by the school you attended with the subjects of study you listed, such as history of Russia from the ninth to the nineteenth centuries, history of ancient Greece and Rome, philosophy, logic, Russian literature, French literature, and French language. You took four semesters of courses in the years 1915, 1916, and 1917, at which time your life was changed forever by the volcanic upheaval of the so-called Socialist/Proletarian Revolution. The fire of violence spread through this enormous land of Eurasia, fueled by hunger and ages of injustices, as well as by the propaganda of lofty promises of giving everybody, as the Marxist/Communistic ideal promised, "to each according to their needs" and requesting "from each according to their abilities." It never happened, and finally after almost three-quarters of a century of cruel dictatorship, it all fell apart, plunging your motherland into another kind of chaos.

I'm writing about all of these circumstances, not because my intention, dear Olik, is to write a history book—there are many of them, much better than I could ever write. My intention is to give a background, as painters do, to emphasize the main subject of their composition, to create a scenery behind the painting, a total being the sum of experienced perception.

◆   ◆   ◆   ◆

So here I was: a very young girl unaware at the time of all this world-changing history, coming into your life with my own heavy, twelve-year-old ballast of mind-shattering history, a traveler with luggage full of a different background and experiences. You understood from the beginning that reconciliation of our two different worlds would be a process and not a sudden, magical switch. And so it was.

◆   ◆   ◆   ◆

Before I go any further into the story of our life together, I want to tell you that in this moment of quiet evening I have in front of me two photographs of you. Usually they are standing on the bookshelf of my bedroom next to the pictures of Mama with Janka, my children and grandchildren. But right now, I put those two photographs in front of me to help the river of memories and the tributaries of emotions to flood, to embrace and nourish all the feelings I have about you and hold dear.

◆　◆　◆　◆

It is a November night outside; the sky is covered with heavy, low clouds, and gentle drops of rain are falling with a clicking noise on the sturdy, fan-shaped leaves of a palm in front of my window, and the paysage, as the French would say, couldn't be more different from the winter night I met you.

Together with me, looking at me from your photograph as I listen to raindrops of time, is a beautiful woman, probably in her mid- to late twenties, with a perfect oval-shaped face, dark hair, and dark brown eyes framed with delicate arches of eyebrows. She is dressed in a silky white blouse, her shoulders caught by the camera in profile while her head is turned toward me—en face, again as the French would say. The heart-shaped lips are open slightly in a delicate half-smile. Knowing the masters of Russian literature, to whom you, dear Olga, introduced me with such fervent passion and whom I learned to admire, this woman looking at me from the sepia-colored photograph could be a heroine in their stories. She could be in Chekhov's plays, in his or Turgenev's short stories; she could be Anna Karenina or Tatiana in Pushkin's Evgeny Onegin. But fate had different plans for her. Even the Gypsy women I knew in my childhood, with their great imagination and fantasy, would not be able to predict her future.

In the other photograph, made in 1945 in Penza, is an image of you and me. You are sitting, and I'm standing very close to you. By this time you are forty-nine years old, and I am thirteen. You are still beautiful, but your hair is silvery gray. The girl—that is, me—has a sweet but rather serious expression of face, almost adultlike. Also in this picture is one thing that nobody would ever notice but I remember very well. Pinned to my sweater is a thin golden brooch in a shape of a safety pin with a pea-sized green jade stone in the middle. This was a gift from you—the first piece of jewelry I ever had and thus memorable even now. This picture was made during the one year we were alone together, only the two of us. Papa was moving with his army hospital toward the Western Front in the rear of the advancing army. This was the time when the bond between us started to develop. Over the next twenty years it grew into a love that I continue to cherish.

· · · ·

That night Papa first introduced you to me I made a curtsy—in Polish it was called a dyg—as I was taught long ago, before the war, to make when I was greeting an adult. May I digress to say that many customs like that are out of fashion now? Similarly, it has become the way of the past for a man greeting a woman to place a kiss on her hand. This custom persisted, however, throughout my life until I left Poland in 1968. As a matter of fact, that gesture was accompanied by saying, "Caluje raczki," "I kiss your little hands," which very often substituted for "Good morning," "Good day," "Good-bye," or any other greeting of a woman by a man. After introducing you to me, Papa then said, "and this my daughter Helunia" and then he added, "Lenochka," in Russian.

I think you were surprised by my curtsy, since it was an anachronism and definitely out of place in postrevolutionary Russia. Along with the surprise on your face, I also noticed a warm and inviting smile. This was our introduction to each other. I was very tired; the long trip and cramped-up emotions finally took a toll. I remember I had a hot glass of milk with sweet breadlike cake. I remember Papa was translating words exchanged between you and me. I don't know how long this "conscious" evening lasted, but the next thing I remember, I was in my bed and you were covering me with a woolen blanket. There is no dream I remember from that first night, but I have the blanket with me here in California. You knitted this blanket for me while you waited for my arrival. I wonder what you were thinking in those hours as you knitted? I know now, from experience and from your own confessions, that your thoughts were akin to thoughts of all mothers expecting a child to arrive into their life. But your experience of anticipated motherhood was not an ordinary one, one repeated by biological laws from the beginning of time. You were waiting for a gift of fate, which until now had not been generous to you.

This "gift of fate" arrived at the doorstep of your heart in a twelve-year-old package that opened to a handful of trouble. You opened this package layer by layer, with patience, sensitivity, and love, sometimes with tears of sadness but always with faith and determination to achieve a beneficial outcome for both of us.

◆ ◆ ◆ ◆

The first days with you were immersed in the superficiality of ordinary daily needs. I needed new clothes for the harsh winter and most of all I needed new shoes suited for temperatures of forty below—>Centigrade, that is. You procured them for me in a short few days through your special connections, which wasn't an easy task in Russia during that time. The shoes I got were called valonky. They were ugly, but heaven for my feet. Valonky were made of thick, brown, pure wool felt, shaped while wet on different-sized forms resembling a human foot and then extended from ankle to knee in a wide tube. When the process was finished, what came out of it was a stiff, pure wool boot. Everybody was wearing them, including the Russian army.

There was no worry about them getting wet, because at no time during the winter would the snow be melting. Snow was as hard and dry as white cement. To clear the sidewalks or a path to the house, a miner's pickax had to be used. Having those oven-like boots and warm clothes, I started to enjoy this unusual winter. We shopped for food in small, open peasants' markets, where all kinds of produce were available. The surrounding villages were all so-called kolchozy—government-imposed "collective farms"—but each peasant family was allowed to have a small field and garden around the house, and a cow and some chickens. In actuality, those small private enterprises were feeding provincial Russia. The governmental food stores were almost always empty, and when occasional food was delivered to them, the queues were endlessly long. Often when one reached the counter, the produce was gone.

◆ ◆ ◆ ◆

I spent all of my time with you. I was asleep when Papa left for work and when he came back from the military hospital. Sometimes he didn't come home for a few days, and occasionally for a week or so. During those longer absences, he and a group of nurses from his hospital went to attend sick German soldiers tucked away in a POW camp deep in the forests between Penza and Kazan. Many years later I learned from Papa how appalling their conditions were in those POW camps. I remember you saying, after learning my war story, that they deserved no better.

◆ ◆ ◆ ◆

In the meantime, in a few weeks I learned enough of the Russian language to communicate with you and the other children who lived in the same house. You didn't have children's books, so you read to me and taught me to read the most beautiful examples of Russian literature. Pushkin's fairytale "Ruslan and Ludmila" was my favorite.

◆ ◆ ◆ ◆

As the daily routine settled down among the three of us, almost suddenly one day it came to the surface of my consciousness that all of us, including me, had forgotten the person I loved the most—my mother. I suddenly felt guilty for starting to be happy again. I didn't know whom to blame, Papa or you. He was my father, the anchor to the past; you were a stranger. It was easier to blame you. Now that I was a real child again, being well taken care of, I was able to ask the obvious question: Who is this woman?

Children are not small adults. They have their own psychological logic of reasoning. I became resentful of Papa, outwardly hostile to you. He was my father, but you were a stranger who dared to replace my Mama. I was old enough to understand that you lived as husband and wife, although you were not married and carried different last names.

There were days I didn't speak to you, did not answer your questions or greetings or respond to your attempts to be close to me. I obeyed the rules of the household silently and reluctantly. It must have been heart-wrenching for you, but you never lost your patience though I know you shed tears of sadness secretly.

It's too late in my life and pointless to be judgmental about Papa. The only point I now want to make in this letter to you, dear Olik, is that you, Olga Aleksandrovna, your persona, your love, and your loyalty, were a redemption to his trespass.

◆　◆　◆　◆

My trespass in turn was a desire for exclusivity. I wanted exclusive love from him. There was no room in my greedy desire for a trio. Supported by an injured heart, in my childish egoism, I didn't realize that you were offering me your exclusive love and attention, willing to endure the lack of reciprocity, somehow believing in its transience.

◆　◆　◆　◆

There were three moments in our life in Penza, which, besides your steady course in taming my anger, helped to calm my soul and open the gate for something better than anger to come. I will tell you about these moments in order of their importance to my gradually growing warmth toward you.

The first was on a Sunday. Papa was not working and you arranged, again through your connection with people who knew you and your family from long ago, a horse-drawn sleigh to take us on an outing for a day. It was cold, but the sky was turquoise blue and the sun was blindingly bright. It took us about two hours of the horse's trotting to get to a place of magical beauty. We were standing on the banks of a big river, which we had just crossed. The river's surface was still covered with thick ice and snow and the sun was making rainbow-colored sparkles on the ice. There were small undulating hills on both sides of the river, covered here and there with clumps of pines. In contrast to this dreamlike whiteness and shine, the trees looked black, and only when you came close to them could you recognize the usual greenness of the pine needles. Sometimes the road would turn into a white crystal tunnel with snow walls almost two meters high on both sides. I was sitting between the two of you, happy to talk and laugh while embraced by such celestial and earthly magic. On the way back home, not far from the city, we suddenly heard a repeated high-pitched yelp. We stopped and, on foot, all moved toward the desperate yap. Tangled in the branches of a small, leafless bush was a little white pup. You, Olik, picked him up and put him in my arms. He was a skinny, trembling, dirty-white little ball of flesh with black eyes and a pink tongue. There was no doubt that we would take him with us, but there were a lot of doubts as to whether or not I could keep him. My father had plenty of arguments why we shouldn't; all of them were reasonably valid in his mind, but none in my mind. In a desperate desire to have this pup, I squeezed your hand, and you returned the gesture, which was a sign of our secret understanding. Until that time you hadn't said a word, but then you turned to me with a smile and a wink. You then proceeded to convince Papa what a good thing it would be for me to have him. We won. You and I became closer than ever before in this moment. When we returned home I washed him and fed him and named him Sniezhok, "snowflake."

He slept with me and never left my side until 1946, when, with tears and heartache, I had to give him up before we left for Poland. My friend, a boy who lived in the same house, was happy to inherit Sniezhok and promised to take good care of him. I hope he did.

•   •   •   •

One day you asked me if I had ever seen a museum. This was the second moment. Not only had I never seen one, I didn't even know what a museum was. So the next day you took me to the only one existing in the city of Penza. It was a big building with an impressive front portico and wide steps leading to a colonnaded entrance. It was a palace that had been confiscated from a local aristocrat and nationalized by the state. The aristocrat's private objects of art were now the contents of this museum.

The general atmosphere of veneration of art made a bigger impression on me than the art itself, although I remember one sculpture of a woman with a little baby in her arms that I really liked. We walked some time through the numerous rooms of the museum and somehow got separated by a big group of schoolchildren. I lost sight of you. I kept walking faster and faster through the rooms, with some panic and anxiety, not knowing what to do, when I heard an announcement on the loud speaker mentioning my name. What I heard was that Lenochka, the daughter of Olga Aleksandrowna, should go to the "blue room," where her mother was waiting for her. It was an easy task, and I found you. What remained ringing in my ears was the loud announcement, symbolically to the whole world, that I was your daughter and that we were not going to lose each other. This was an affirmation for both of us, and especially for me that I belonged and that you would make it happen.

◆　◆　◆　◆

The third moment was this: One gloomy, lazy day, we stayed home, lingering in our beds after Papa went to work. On that day, after many weeks of being together, I sat on the edge of your bed and answered your cautious questions about my life before the war. You and Papa never induced me to talk about my horrifying lonely years—you waited patiently for my readiness to talk about it. Occasionally bits and pieces came out of me as a matter of fact, but for the full account you had to wait many years. Even then it was sporadic, until now.

I guess in a way I was lucky to have been a child in those times. Children have a higher ability to recover from unusual circumstances. They respond to the basic reflexes of survival rather than intellectually analyzing the suffering and the worth of life after it. I know of some people who ended their lives by suicide, unable to cope with their memories. A famous example is Primo Levi, the Italian writer. Relentless philosophical dissection and a search for explanations must have led him to suicide. It is possible to heal if one can find a noble side of humanity. Sometimes music, poetry, paintings, and literature have a great power of healing and of giving hope.

I'm sorry, my dear Olga, for this unexpected diversion from what I really wanted to remind you of concerning that gloomy, lazy day of our intimate talk.

You asked me to tell you about some pleasurable things I remembered that I liked to do. For some reason I chose to tell you about my ballet lessons and you asked me if I would show you how I could dance. To make it more real and theatrical, you got out of bed and opened a big trunk standing in the corner from which you took a beautiful long dress with a wavy design in pink, gray, and orange. It was silky and long, and when I put it on, it flowed with the motion of my body. It had two jeweled silver buttons with turquoise stones in the middle sewn into the bodice, the close-fitting top of the dress. You told me it was a gift to you from your father, when long ago he had bought it for you on his journey to Turkey, and that now it would be mine. As you know, I used it until the silk fell apart after many washings. Many years later, you made two silver rings from the jeweled buttons, one for your sister Nina and one for me. I still have it and wear it often, one more tangible memory of you.

So, all dressed up in this Turkish gown, I danced for you an imaginary dance of a harem, as you called it. When I finished, tired of dancing between the furniture of our crowded room, I jumped on your bed. We both laughed at our simple enjoyment of it all. You embraced me and kissed me, and we stayed in this embrace for a while in silence. When I turned my face toward yours, I saw silent tears coming down your cheeks. I sat up and slowly dried your tears with my hands.

In this mixture of child and adult that was in me at the time, I realized that to complete the bond between us I needed to tell you about that last moment I saw my mother, when she begged a strange woman to take me as her daughter and save me from the destruction to which she was forced a few seconds later.

After I finished my story, you told me in your soft Russian words, that I would be your daughter forever and you would love me even longer than forever and that to honor my mother, her sacrifice, and her gift to you, I should call you by your name, Olga, meaning you would not expect me to call you "Mama." How noble and sweet it was of you to say it. This was the moment I realized that I was blessed, as only few people are, with two mothers in one life—the mother that gave me the gift of life twice, and you, my dearest Olik. You kept your promise to the end of your life, indulging me with your unconditional love. You repeated in words to whomever wanted to listen and in your actions that I could never do any wrong in your eyes. You let me know throughout our life together that I was the star in your sky. And yes, you spoiled me as much as you could with material things, as well as with the largesse of your feelings.

◆　◆　◆　◆

The winter was still raging on. In this part of the world the earth was frozen hard, the snow was falling daily, and strong eastern winds were blowing heaps of snow from place to place, shaping them like dunes of sands are shaped by winds in the Sahara desert. And yes, the temperatures often reached forty below.

People were going to work, getting out of their houses, the doors of which were sometimes invisible, buried under the snow. Children went to school dressed in heavy woolen or fur coats and fur hats. And I was one of them. I mastered the Russian language well enough to be signed up to the fifth grade, which was not bad—I was behind only one grade for my age. At that time, the Russian school system had ten grades, equivalent to twelve grades here. After graduating from tenth grade, one could start a university education. My main education, however, was at home. Papa was working long hours, so his tutoring was always on Sundays. I had a lot of catching up to do with all the subjects I had never heard of before, such as botany, biology, algebra, history, literature, and geography. You both realized that for me to fall into a fixed routine of schooling I would need some more time and help. My favored subjects were literature and geography. I suddenly discovered how grandiose this planet Earth is—with oceans and continents and mountains full of exotic names and people. All of this colorful imagery was almost like a fairytale, making me occasionally doubt if it really existed. I learned from you that Penza, the town we lived in, located about seven hundred kilometers southeast of Moscow, was the capital of the Mordvinian Autonomic Republic and that people I met on the streets and in surrounding villages were called Mordva in Russian.

They were stocky people, with a slightly yellowish hue of skin, hazel-colored eyes, and brown hair. You thought they were of Mongolian descent, the majority of them working in the fields. I think you would be surprised to know what I just recently learned, that Mordvinians were one of the ancient Finno-Ugric tribes scattered throughout the Russian land west of the Ural Mountains as far away as west of the Volga River. They were once great people, masters of agriculture. They spoke a language closely related to Finnish and Hungarian, their cousins, and the census of 1897 counted their number at more than one million. They were decimated, and many were resettled to Siberia, by Stalin, who feared any cohesive ethnic group. I have some good memories of visiting with a Mordvinian peasant family—a daughter of your nanny, who was about your age—and you shared fond memories of both of your mothers. She treated us with good and plentiful food and, as in old prerevolutionary Russia, she bowed deeply when greeting you, making the usual triple signs of the cross on the chest, as all observant Russian Orthodox do.

✦　✦　✦　✦

Some months after I started school, Papa left us, going west with the Russian army hospital. Only sporadic letters from him told us that he was alive, but army secrecy did not allow him to tell us his location.

I didn't make any friends in school, being a little older than the rest of my class and a bit of an outsider. Your main reason for sending me to school was to "normalize" my life by giving me contact with my peers. Since that was a failure, you took me out of school. Again, as once before in my life, my protector became my teacher.

✦　✦　✦　✦

The warm winds of spring announced themselves in late March with rainy days here and there, and by April the greenery of trees and grasses exploded around us with delicate, pastel colors of baby leaves and faint contours of buds. As in any cold climate, Nature doesn't waste time and rushes to fulfill the promise of renewal. Even in these hard times, people responded to spring with smiles on their pale faces, and through open windows one could hear children's voices and the songs of their mothers. This great symphony of colors and sounds came to a triumphant finale: on May 9, 1945, the war ended.

The official and private jubilation of that day were all around us, pounding our senses. Our joy was more than bittersweet; it came with the inevitable sorrows for lives lost. There were times, mostly in the night hours, when I felt enormous guilt at being alive while those I loved had perished.

You heard my night cries and would run to comfort me with your love. You explained to me that if I lived my life well and happily, the spirits of my mother and sister, their spirits and intentions, their life-giving forces, would reside in my soul and mind forever. You and my little white pup, Sniezhok, were the best psychologists and healers of my wounds.

My dear Olik, you would most certainly be surprised and incredulous if I told you how many people I knew and how many patients I had who spent many years and much money in the quest of "curing" their egocentric and self-indulgent ideas of suffering. In many instances, a simple reversal of giving instead of taking would have helped them. Some of those diseases that became truly life-threatening, such as anorexia nervosa, you would dismiss in one short Russian proverb, Ot jirou biesatsa, "They get crazy because of too much fat," fat in this instance meaning too many goods, too much of everything coming in an easy way. Nobody had this disease during the war in our part of the world, or in the concentration camps, or in the ghetto where I lived, and I'm sure nobody has it nowadays in starving Ethiopia or Sudan. So much for our times. O tempora, o mores!

* * * *

One day we got a letter from Papa, saying that he would come back and take us both to Poland, but it would not be for at least six or twelve months. The two of you arranged to be married in the city hall of Penza just before he left. There were no ceremonies or parties to commemorate that event, just an official piece of paper that changed your old surname to a new one. This gave you the right to receive a monthly stipend from the Russian Army as the wife of an officer-physician. That money, plus old family treasures you occasionally sold, provided for us what I remember as a comfortable sustenance.

* * * *

On a day that you came home from some errand in the city, you presented me with a beautiful, silky, dark blue skirt and white blouse with long sleeves and a stand-up collar, typical for a Russian man's shirt but this one dainty and made of lace. You told me that we were going to dress up, both of us, and go to the theater. You bought tickets for us, standing almost two hours in line, to see an operetta given by an ensemble of actors and singers who came to Penza from Kazan, a bigger city not far away. Of course I didn't know what an operetta was, but I was in a few hours to learn what a delightful experience it would be. It wasn't my first encounter with music, and Papa's piano performances in my childhood were still memorable imprints of my fantasy world. But this was different. This was fantasy incarnate! It engaged all the senses—the actors and singers had exotic costumes, they moved and sang and danced, creating a colorful kaleidoscope with each changing scene. The operetta was called Tzyganskij Baron, composed by Johann Strauss, an Austrian composer. He wrote other operettas during his lifetime and his Viennese waltzes enchanted millions throughout the world and still do. In English, this operetta is called The Gypsy Baron. We walked out of the theater holding hands and singing some of the joyous arias together aloud, not paying attention to people around us. It was a night of the full moon, warm, with a delicate breeze of moving air. When I looked up to the sky I could have sworn that the smiling face of the Earth's companion, the Luna, was giving me a friendly wink and twinkle of her eyes in approval of our joy.

◆ ◆ ◆ ◆

This was just the beginning of new discoveries and adventures you had in mind for me.

You told me that when Papa took us to Poland, you probably would never again see this land of your birth, Russia, so this was perhaps your only chance to make some of your wishes and desires come true. There were three of them. I listened in awe of your unfolding plans. Your pulsating energy kindled my emotions to new and unknown levels.

Number one: we would take a trip to Moscow, where your only remaining family—your sister, Nina, brother, Misha, and niece, Irina—lived. You were also very close to your aunt—your father's sister, Varvara (Barbara) Michajlovna—so we certainly would have some time with her. You wanted me to meet them and to have them share your good fortune of motherhood. Number two: from there we would take a trip to see the beauty of Lake Baikal, which lay far to the east of Moscow, in the south of the vast land of Siberia. Apparently, your father had promised to take you there one day, and never did. The stories he told you about that place never left your imagination, and now you most fervently wanted to share it with me. You didn't know if that dream was attainable, but you would give it your best try. Number three: you wanted to go with me to Crimea, the place of your happiest childhood memories. I understood that dream the best.

You warned me that none of it, or maybe only the voyage to Moscow, might be realized, given the difficulties that such extensive traveling, shortly after the war, would entail. You were amazing in your firmness of purpose—and yes, we did it all. By "we" I mean you arranged it all, but you told me I was the best companion you ever had. Probably my experiences of my life alone, my street smartness combined with the happiness and safety of your protective closeness, made it all more pleasurable than difficult for both of us.

Not to vex your patience, my dear Olik, but I will remind you of only a few moments that revealed the new world around me and brought the richness of perception of it, so far away from the tiny little town of Warez where I spent my happy early childhood—so utterly different from yours.

◆　◆　◆　◆

I know from the conversations between Papa and you and from stories you told me yourself that you loved your country very deeply and with every fiber of your being. This love was independent of political regimes. This land had been yours forever, for uncountable generations. It was blind historical fate that had brought you and this land together and bound you with solemn promises and vows, as in the rites of marriage: "to love and obey, in sickness and in health, till death do us part . . . " You loved the vast expanses of the land, the rivers, mountains, and forests; the talents and romantic voices of the poets; the mystic, haunting music; the sometimes healing, sometimes wounding genius of your writers; the painters who put on canvas what you knew from life or from books describing the turbulent history of your land and its people; the spontaneous, unschooled, but perfect peasant songs, spreading over the rivers on moonlit nights. Those songs echo in my consciousness now, in the same way as the blues born in the souls of the American Negro slaves. They both sound like a cry or a prayer of submission to a higher power, beyond human control. When the pain is too much to bear, the music and the songs burst into a fire of rhythmic, joyous sounds of dance. It is a sound not only of dreams of joy but also of rebellion. I thank you now, for conveying to me this love of yours for matters higher than easy life and material possessions. From the perspective of old age, I understand and value it more than ever before.

◆　◆　◆　◆

It was after a relatively short trip by train that we reached Moscow, greeted by your sister Nina and her husband Jura. It was daytime when we arrived and the only way to get to their house was by an electric trolley bus. Aunt Nina and Uncle Jura protected me from the pushing crowds of people as if I were a porcelain doll—they had never had children and they didn't know my story, so they didn't know that by this time I felt unbreakable. Oh, the arrogance of youth!

The trolley bus was a vehicle on rubber wheels, powered by electricity via D-shaped metal pipes over the roof of the bus sliding under thick, electric wires hanging in the air. From the window of the trolley I saw thick masses of people walking in all directions to unknown destinations. Very few cars or trucks passed by. The day was gray and cloudy, the people's clothes were dark, and only here and there young girls, as if to greet the spring, tried to beautify the streets with some color in their scarves and hats.

The house your sister lived in was a tall building, with two large apartments on each floor. Before the revolution, each apartment had been occupied by a single, probably well-to-do family. Now they housed one family in each room, sharing one kitchen and a couple of bathrooms. The food was scarce in the capital of Russia at the end of the war, little more plentiful than during the dark and frozen times of the war. The one thing in abundance was vodka. If not the refined kind, there was always samogon, moonshine.

Nevertheless, by sheer magic, or rather by the use of her survival skills developed over the years of deprivation, Aunt Nina procured a feast and invited all the members of your family living in Moscow to celebrate.

I met them all on that first (but not last) visit to Moscow, even your first husband, from whom you had already been divorced for several years. He was a very handsome, tall man with very black hair, dark brooding eyes, and somewhat exotic facial features. He now had a new wife and a child. Much later in time, when I was already an adult woman, during one of our heart-to-heart talks you gave me many hints that the reason for your parting was your inability to have children. Thinking now about it, with contemporary knowledge of genetics, it is possible that some faulty gene was passed, maybe from your paternal grandmother to the women of the next two generations—to your aunts, sisters of your father who never had children, and to you and your sister Nina, who were also marked with this inability.

The only child in your family was Irina, a daughter of your brother Misha; she was one year younger than I, and she sat next to me at the feast prepared for us by Nina for Sunday dinner.

The food preparations took two days of kitchen labor. Only two gas burners and one oven shared with the other tenants were at Nina's disposal. That was the easiest part. The most difficult, which took two weeks, was procuring the raw material for the feast, an achievement that only your sister knew how to accomplish. The menu was traditional, typical Russian. When the table was set on Sunday afternoon, it was graced with colors and shapes I had never seen before: there was a black and red caviar from the Caspian Sea; there was a whole roasted piglet with a carrot in his snout; there was cabbage stew and red cabbage with a white onion–vinaigrette salad sprinkled with wine; there were red, almost purple beets with white bubbles of sour cream on each slice; there were sliced and fried potatoes freckled with ground pepper; there was roasted beef covered with thick golden-brown gravy and home-baked bread with a divine aroma and crunchy crust.

tortured souls, without a Dante to sing about it until the time of Solzhenitsyn's Gulag Archipelago. After several years, Tina-Ar was allowed to come back from Siberia, broken in body and spirit, but was forbidden ever to return to Moscow. She died shortly thereafter in a faraway village, in the arms of her bohemian lover, now an old man.

There are many ways that those who fear losing absolute power can spread the plague of injustice and irreversibly change a promising life, throwing it into an abyss of despair. Your brother Misha was an example of this. He was a beautiful boy, the youngest in the family, spoiled first by your mother and then by two loving sisters. Intelligent and talented, he became a physicist, graduating from Moscow University. To everybody's surprise, he married a Jewish girl of very average appearance—and this was the reason for surprise, since he was considered always a ladies' man, never lacking the companionship of young beauties. Less than a year later, his daughter was born, a blonde, blue-eyed girl whom he adored. He was working in the Physics Department of the Academy of Science and progressed rapidly to an important position. The secrecy of this position almost completely isolated him from his family and friends. He lived and worked behind high walls in an Institute of Physics, as it was called, hidden away in the forest in the vicinity of Moscow. Within a short time the rules tightened, and he was allowed to visit his wife and child only once a month. Within two years the family fell apart—his wife divorced him. He could see his daughter on Sundays only if she could be transported to him for a visit. As the years moved forward, the visits became ever so rare. He lived a lonely life in a comfortable jail. But a jail is a jail even by another name.

In his lonely hours of depression, he turned to the only friendly remedy available, alcohol, which gave him a semblance of reprieve from his ever-growing sadness. For every outing from this place he lived, he had to apply for special permission, and even then he was followed and watched by the secret police. Aunt Nina told us—you and me—about it many years later. You knew, dear Olik, that our Sunday feast would be the last time you would see your brother. Your parting was tearful and almost ghostly. Your handsome, talented, beloved brother Misha died in his early fifties from the consequences of chronic alcoholism.

It is true that vodka isn't only a remedy of choice for a slow suicide. Maybe a rapid one would seem more noble. But I refuse to give the right of judgment to anybody who has not experienced a life without freedom.

I know that you, Olik, would agree with me.

I don't remember who wrote this poem, which I want now to quote in memory of many Russian Mishas and Tina-Ars. I'll probably not be exact in my transcription, but I know you'll excuse my deficient memory. As I recall, it was directed to a woman loved by this poet. I will direct it to Lady Freedom and do my best to convey the spirit of it—so here it is:

> Though great my errors, great has been my grief,
> And one looked to you for some relief,
> Think then in pity, love and tender care
> Upon the suffering I'm left to bear,
> And seek to set a wretched soul free,
> Who loses so much in losing thee.

◆　◆　◆　◆

As I'm recalling this time with you in my budding teens, many "firsts" were unfolding for me in rapid succession. I was soaking them in as parched soil absorbs the heavenly rain and hastens to revive the dormant seeds, transforming them into green fields of grass and rainbow colors of flowers.

For me, there were first poets and storytellers in a new language, there were first museums showing human history in art, there were freezing winds never experienced before, there was a first operetta with the infectious gaiety I never suspected music could evoke, and now came another first.

A few days after our Sunday feast, you took me to the Bolshoi, the famous Moscow theater, where the ballet Sleeping Beauty was presented. The story was told by magnificent dancers, men and women, to the music of Tchaikovsky. How could a tormented man bring out of his mind such mesmerizing sounds? Maybe the release of beauty is always compelled by a torment of one sort or another?

◆　◆　◆　◆

A week or so later, we were on our way to Baikal, the sixth-largest and the deepest lake in the world, spreading its waters in the southeast of the Asiatic part of Russia. The Mongols call it Dalai-nor; the Turks, Baj-kul. It is frozen solid from December until late April. The lake has a romantic resonance in the Russian psyche. It was discovered in the mid-seventeenth century, and by the end of the nineteenth century adventurous travelers had described its physical features and surrounding mountains, rivers, and fauna. When the great trans-Siberian railroad, connecting the European part of Russia with the Pacific shores of the Far East, was finished in 1905, this unique natural beauty was open to those who had money and time to admire it, or to those who were forced to pioneer this land. I never told you this before, but as a sixteen-year-old girl, attending high school in Warsaw, I met an old man who was a great uncle of my best friend at the time. He had been a Polish civil engineer recruited by the Russians when the tsars were the lords of Poland, and he spent many years as one of the builders of the railroad. He returned home a rich man clad in sable furs and gold, and used to tell us phantasmagoric stories about his life in this vast land of Siberia.

This was our second day on the road; we had a fairly comfortable railroad car with two bunk beds and a bench all to ourselves. You later told me that it took a lot of bribing of people in influential places and some liquidation of your jewelry not only to achieve this comfort, but most importantly to obtain a permit for the two of us to travel. Everyone in Russia held a passport. Free movement at will from place to place was not allowed. In this proletarian paradise, one had to register with the police at his place of departure and report to the police station at his destination. This strict police surveillance of the movement of the population continued well past Stalin's death.

But never mind all this; let's go to my next first. This time it was travel for travel's sake, for the pleasure of awakening each day in a different place—not travel to escape danger, not even travel to find a lost father. Just travel! The train moved swiftly; the stops were infrequent at small outposts.

Although it was spring, in the wee hours of the morning the Siberian steppes, stretching from the Ural Mountains to the Pacific, were covered with opalescent fog, which rolled over the pale green earth and the still cold, black waters of the rivers we passed. In those eerily bleak expanses, we rarely saw people, who only occasionally gathered at train stops. Our first destination was the city of Irkutsk; from there we would make our way to Baikal. When we finally reached the lake, we passed through, if I remember well, four time zones, bringing the next two firsts for me. I had to change the time on my first wristwatch four times! The watch was a gift from Papa, who bought it for me in Penza from a watchmaker who stole the parts from a watch factory where he worked. He supplemented his income by assembling watches from these parts and selling them on the black market. The name of the watch was Penza, but don't worry, Switzerland; this trademark will always be obscure to the world and will cause you no competitive headaches.

This first, the wristwatch, was connected to the concept of time zones—ergo the next first. The concept of the trick that Mother Earth played on me, rotating on its own axis in addition to orbiting the sun, was definitely over my head. The only certain and familiar thing for me was that each day started with sunrise and ended with sunset.

I must confess to you, my dear Olik, that even now I have to concentrate my mind not to confuse the time zones between the west and east. My naïve and honest admission of this particular deficiency brings an ironic but sympathetic smile to my husband Jan's face, which he follows immediately with an explanation of the "relativity" of time. Yes, he is the same Jan you knew in Warsaw at the time we started to plan our life together.

But all that aside, you and I both knew that we understood for sure the song of birds, to which we listened sitting in front of the fisherman's cabin where we stayed on the shore of the lake Baikal. The birds came over the lake in waves that darkened the skies. This was their triumphant song of life after the thick ice covering Baikal for the winter months finally melted and the birds' feeding frenzy could begin. The mountains on the eastern shore of Baikal were only visible on sunny days from twenty-five to fifty kilometers across the water. We ate a lot of fish and ventured out in our host's fishing boat only on calm and sunny days. On rainy days we stayed in the cabin, listening to the fisherman's son playing the balalaika while his younger brother was teaching me how to play the game of checkers—another first for me. I will not bore you with all my future firsts. They are, after all, a natural occurrence in any growing child's life. There is a funny, romantic side to them, one of them being that I never met another person in my life who learned to play checkers on the shores of Lake Baikal, taught by a boy of half-Mongolian, half-Turkish ancestry.

♦ ♦ ♦ ♦

We returned to Penza in late June. It took some time, even with your high enterprising spirit and talent, to navigate through the labyrinths of Soviet bureaucracy to arrange our trip to Crimea. But we made it.

I will not bore you with my childish enchantment with this place, because I know you were sadly disappointed with its degradation: dilapidated palaces, the gray crowds of people, and the absence of the glory of this corner of your country. For me it was an endless wonderment of changing views and exotic names on maps coming to life. We reached Rostov on the Don River. The names of cities with the attachment of a river to them, like Stratford-upon-Avon or Frankfurt am Main, had a rhythm to them as if a poetic saga should immediately follow. We then brushed the western slopes of the Caucasus Mountains, and, after crossing a narrow strait of the Sea of Azov, ended our journey in famous Yalta. If I had the power of giving names to earthly places, the Black Sea would be called the Lapis Lazuli Sea, for the color of its waters appeared to me as melted lapis with golden sparks of the sun's rays bursting here and there. I know we stayed in Yalta much longer than you wanted, only because you saw in my eyes the endless delight in the sensation of discovery. On my own microscopic scale I was having moments worthy of Vasco da Gama or Captain Cook.

We returned to Odessa, bypassing Rostov, once the capital of mighty Cossacks, and were back in a short time in Penza, which seemed so drab and dull now, as indeed it was.

The year 1946 was upon us, and we had only a few months to close up your household and pack the belongings we were allowed to take with us to our new destination—Warsaw, liberated from German occupation. Papa was soon coming to take us there.

I was your main helper in those preparations, and by the end I became an expert packer, as you named me—by your own admission much better than you. Funny, but true. I must tell you, my dear Olik, that this expertise became very handy in my future movement about the globe.

We had to sell all your furniture, some of which were valuable antiques belonging once to your parents. We sold them at the open-air bazaar, held once a week in the middle of the city. Sometimes you had to leave me alone there with our merchandise to mind the selling, and I held firm and steady to my suddenly acquired vendor's position. I never let a canny or shrewd buyer think that a young girl was easy prey for bargains, to allow him to get the desired object for less than the value you assigned to it.

At the end of the day, we both laughed, recounting my street smartness and your soft hands. Petting my cheeks and head, you acknowledged that this cocky ability came from my lonely days not so long ago.

◆　◆　◆　◆

We were ready for our journey to Poland when Papa came to take us to the west. He arranged our trip to include a stop in Lvov with the desire to find at least the nuns who had helped me survive, and who, he knew from the letters sent to us, had themselves survived the war. He wanted to show his gratitude not only in words, but in any other way he could be of help. The nuns, however, were gone, evacuated to western Poland. Kazia, the prostitute with a golden heart, had vanished from the city as well, remaining only in my memory.

For you, the city of Lvov was connected only with me and my family's history, and although you found it beautiful as a landmark, you were anxious to leave it behind.

◆　◆　◆　◆

In the middle of autumn 1946, we crossed the Vistula River to settle in Warsaw, to start our life together anew. Thus, it was the beginning of a new stage in my life as well. I was fourteen years old.

In the ensuing formative years of my adolescence, leading to the maturity of womanhood, your influence on my psyche cannot be exaggerated. So before I finish this letter to you, I ask you to accept my homage and gratitude for all the good that is in me. For the foolish side of my ego, I will be responsible myself.

I thank you for your unconditional love.

I thank you for making me the most important person in your life.

I thank you for your continuous desire to make me happy.

I thank you for your exaggerated opinion that almost no one else could equal me in mind, soul, and body, and even if I took it with a grain of salt, it was a balm to my heart.

I thank you for your pride in my achievements.

I thank you for being an adoring grandmother to my daughters, unfortunately for only a miniscule time to the younger one.

And I thank my lucky stars for bestowing on me the love of two mothers. Although I never called you Mama, you know, my dearest Olik, that you were one, and that I never took you for granted.

◆　◆　◆　◆

You died suddenly but peacefully in 1968 at the age of seventy-two, but as you can see from this long letter, you are alive through me and not forgotten.

Shortly after your death, I left the country of my birth forever, embarking with my newly formed family on the next adventure for many years to come.

Before I left, however, I realized through curious experiences, that when someone dies, sometimes they don't die all at once. They die in pieces: the scent of your perfumes lingered around the house; the mail kept coming in your name; your chair at the table stood there empty as if waiting for you; the comb in front of the mirror had your silver hair entangled in it; and in the evenings I took your favored mohair shawl to embrace my shoulders. These signs of you slowly paved the way to the sweet spirit of tranquility that enfolds me now, where I stand to say good-bye to you.

Your daughter Lenochka

Epilogue

* * * *

So what happened to this little girl who you, the reader of her letters, now knows more intimately?

She got a chance in life and she took it, a chance of life almost like that given to an endangered species.

She grew into a rambunctious teenager. Making up for lost time, she threw herself at the adventures that are life itself, from all-night parties to theater, from dancing to riding motorcycles. She filled her ears with music, from Elvis, whom she idolized, to divine Beethoven's sonatas. She swallowed books in single gulps, from forbidden, trashy erotica to the masterpieces of Émile Zola. She had a hunger for every dish in the worldly meal, and desserts were not to be missed. She discovered romantic, youthful love with the scent of purple lilacs and white jasmines blooming under the starry skies.

As a young woman, she transferred her enthusiasm for life to the profession she loved. The hard work of becoming a doctor became the addiction of lifetime.

There was never too much gray color to her judgments of people or events. Black and white were almost always the favored colors of her opinions.

In a way, she never changed from the girl you met. She just became even more what she had been.

Any later letters to the witnesses of her life, if they are ever written, will still be by the same girl you have learned to know. The important thing that this grown-up and now old girl discovered is that her future would not make much sense, would not be satisfying or filled with hope and possible adventures, if she didn't remember or understand her past.